THIS BOOK IS DEDICATED TO MY LOVING SON ALI AND MY SUPPORTIVE WIFE MASUMA

Contents

Acknowledgements

The completion of this book could not have been possible without the participation and assistance of so many people whose names may not all be enumerated. Their contributions are sincerely appreciated and gratefully acknowledged. However, the group would like to express their deep appreciation and indebtedness particularly to the following:

My students and Colleagues of Dumka Engineering College for their endless support, kind and understanding spirit.

My family, who in one way or another shared their support, either morally, financially and physically, thank you.

Above all, to the Great Almighty, the author of knowledge and wisdom, for his countless love.

Thank you.

Kh. Kamal Ahmed

ONE

MICROPROCESSOR-INTRODUCTION

A microprocessor is a controlling unit of a micro-computer, fabricated on a small chip capable of performing Arithmetic Logical Unit (ALU) operations and communicating with the other devices connected to it.

Microprocessor consists of an ALU, register array, and a control unit. ALU performs arithmetical and logical operations on the data received from the memory or an input device. Register array consists of registers identified by letters like B, C, D, E, H, L and accumulator. The control unit controls the flow of data and instructions within the computer.

Block Diagram of a Basic Microcomputer:

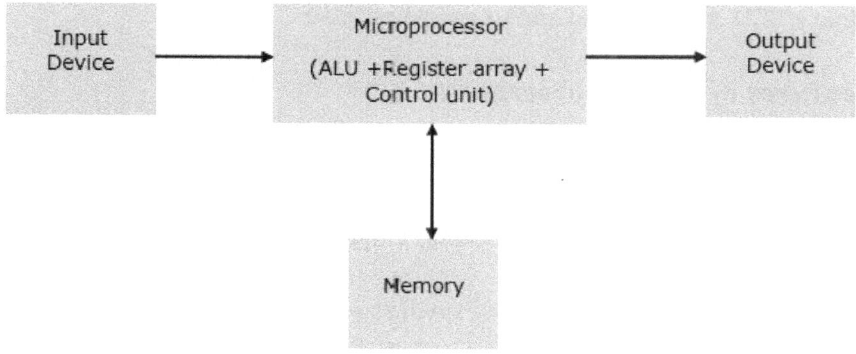

Block Diagram of a Basic Microcomputer

How does a Microprocessor Work?

The microprocessor follows a sequence: Fetch, Decode, and then Execute.

Initially, the instructions are stored in the memory in a sequential order. The microprocessor fetches those instructions from the memory, then decodes it and executes those instructions till STOP instruction is reached. Later, it sends the result in binary to the output port. Between these processes, the register stores the temporarily data and ALU performs the computing functions.

List of Terms Used in a Microprocessor:

Here is a list of some of the frequently used terms in a microprocessor –

Instruction Set – It is the set of instructions that the microprocessor can understand.

Bandwidth – It is the number of bits processed in a single instruction.

Clock Speed – It determines the number of operations per second the processor can perform. It is expressed in megahertz (MHz) or gigahertz (GHz).It is also known as Clock Rate.

Word Length – It depends upon the width of internal data bus, registers, ALU, etc. An 8-bit microprocessor can process 8-bit data at a time. The word length ranges from 4 bits to 64 bits depending upon the type of the microcomputer.

Data Types – The microprocessor has multiple data type formats like binary, BCD, ASCII, signed and unsigned numbers.

Features of a Microprocessor:

Here is a list of some of the most prominent features of any microprocessor –

Cost-effective – The microprocessor chips are available at low prices and results its low cost.

Size – The microprocessor is of small size chip, hence is portable.

Low Power Consumption – Microprocessors are manufactured by using metaloxide semiconductor technology, which has low power consumption.

Versatility – The microprocessors are versatile as we can use the same chip in a number of applications by configuring the software program.

Reliability – The failure rate of an IC in microprocessors is very low, hence it is reliable.

TWO

MICROPROCESSOR - CLASSIFICATION

A microprocessor can be classified into three categories –

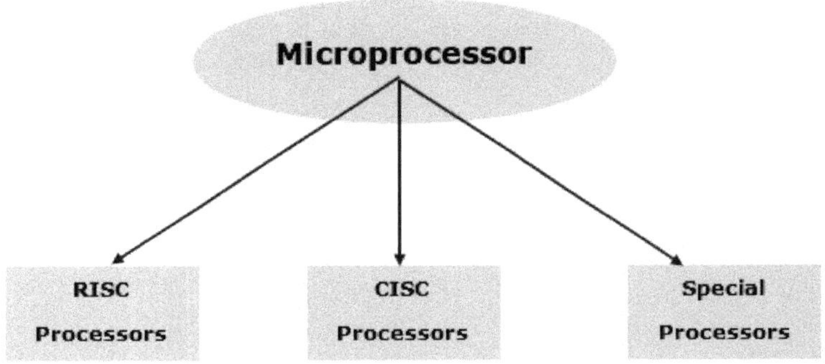

Classification of microprocessor

RISC Processor

RISC stands for Reduced Instruction Set Computer. It is designed to reduce the execution time by simplifying the instruction set of the computer. Using RISC processors, each instruction requires only one clock cycle to execute results in uniform execution time. This reduces the efficiency as there are more lines of code, hence more RAM is needed to store the instructions. The compiler also has to work more to convert high-level language instructions into machine code.

Some of the RISC processors are –

- Power PC: 601, 604, 615, 620
- DEC Alpha: 210642, 211066, 21068, 21164
- MIPS: TS (R10000) RISC Processor
- PA-RISC: HP 7100LC

Architecture of RISC:

RISC microprocessor architecture uses highly-optimized set of instructions. It is used in portable devices like Apple iPod due to its power efficiency.

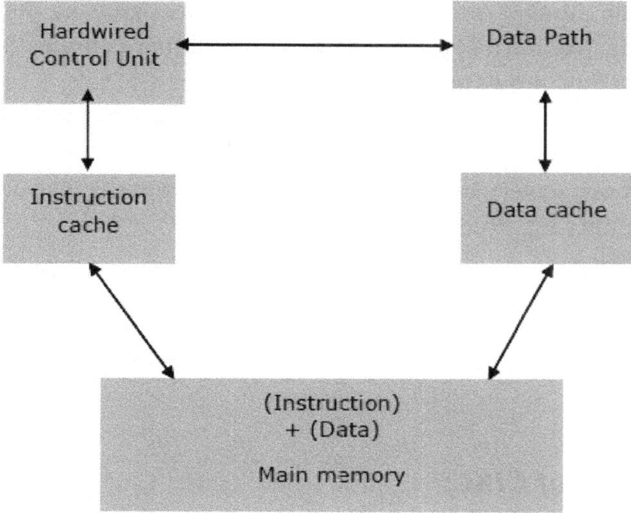

RISC

Characteristics of RISC:

The major characteristics of a RISC processor are as follows –

- It consists of simple instructions.

- It supports various data-type formats.
- It utilizes simple addressing modes and fixed length instructions for pipelining.
- It supports register to use in any context.
- One cycle execution time.
- "LOAD" and "STORE" instructions are used to access the memory location.
- It consists of larger number of registers.
- It consists of less number of transistors.

CISC Processor:

CISC stands for Complex Instruction Set Computer. It is designed to minimize the number of instructions per program, ignoring the number of cycles per instruction. The emphasis is on building complex instructions directly into the hardware.

The compiler has to do very little work to translate a high-level language into assembly level language/machine code because the length of the code is relatively short, so very little RAM is required to store the instructions.

Some of the CISC Processors are –

- IBM 370/168
- VAX 11/780
- Intel 80486

Architecture of CISC:

Its architecture is designed to decrease the memory cost because more storage is needed in larger programs resulting in higher memory cost. To resolve this, the number of instructions per program can be reduced by embedding the number of operations in a single instruction.

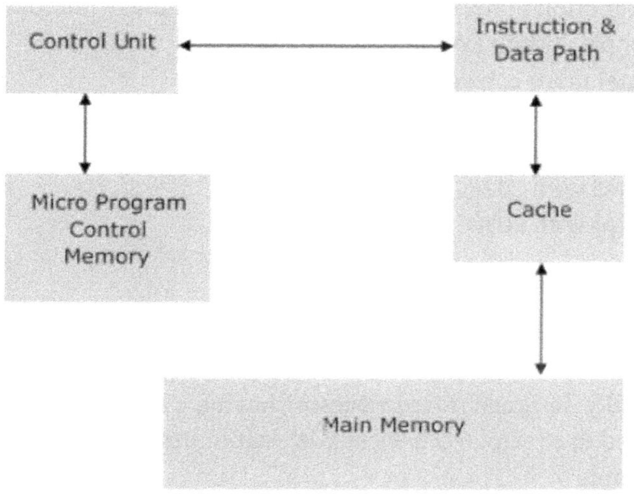

CISC

Characteristics of CISC:

- Variety of addressing modes.
- Larger number of instructions.
- Variable length of instruction formats.
- Several cycles may be required to execute one instruction.
- Instruction-decoding logic is complex.
- One instruction is required to support multiple addressing modes.

Special Processors:

These are the processors which are designed for some special purposes. Few of the special processors are briefly discussed –

Coprocessor:

A coprocessor is a specially designed microprocessor, which can handle its particular function many times faster than the ordinary microprocessor.

For example – Math Coprocessor.

Some Intel math-coprocessors are –

- 8087-used with 8086
- 80287-used with 80286
- 80387-used with 80386

Input/Output Processor:

It is a specially designed microprocessor having a local memory of its own, which is used to control I/O devices with minimum CPU involvement.

For example –

- DMA (direct Memory Access) controller
- Keyboard/mouse controller
- Graphic display controller
- SCSI port controller

Transputer (Transistor Computer):

A transputer is a specially designed microprocessor with its own local memory and having links to connect one transputer to another transputer for inter-processor communications. It was first designed in 1980 by Inmos and is targeted to the utilization of VLSI technology.

A transputer can be used as a single processor system or can be connected to external links, which reduces the construction cost and increases the performance.

For example – 16-bit T212, 32-bit T425, the floating point (T800, T805 & T9000) processors.

DSP (Digital Signal Processor):

This processor is specially designed to process the analog signals into a digital form. This is done by sampling the voltage level at regular time intervals and converting the voltage at that instant into a digital form. This process is performed by a circuit called an analogue to digital converter, A to D converter or ADC.

A DSP contains the following components –

- **Program Memory** – It stores the programs that DSP will use to process data.
- **Data Memory** – It stores the information to be processed.
- **Compute Engine** – It performs the mathematical processing, accessing the program from the program memory and the data from the data memory.
- **Input/Output** – It connects to the outside world.

Its applications are –

- Sound and music synthesis
- Audio and video compression
- Video signal processing
- 2D and 3d graphics acceleration.

For example – Texas Instrument's TMS 320 series, e.g., TMS 320C40, TMS320C50.

THREE

Microprocessor - 8085 Architecture

8085 is pronounced as "eighty-eighty-five" microprocessor. It is an 8-bit microprocessor designed by Intel in 1977 using NMOS technology.

It has the following configuration –

- 8-bit data bus
- 16-bit address bus, which can address upto 64KB
- A 16-bit program counter
- A 16-bit stack pointer
- Six 8-bit registers arranged in pairs: BC, DE, HL
- Requires +5V supply to operate at 3.2 MHZ single phase clock

It is used in washing machines, microwave ovens, mobile phones, etc.

8085 Microprocessor – Functional Units:

8085 consists of the following functional units –

Accumulator

It is an 8-bit register used to perform arithmetic, logical, I/O & LOAD/ STORE operations. It is connected to internal data bus & ALU.

Arithmetic and logic unit

As the name suggests, it performs arithmetic and logical operations like Addition, Subtraction, AND, OR, etc. on 8-bit data.

General purpose register

There are 6 general purpose registers in 8085 processor, i.e. B, C, D, E, H & L. Each register can hold 8-bit data.

These registers can work in pair to hold 16-bit data and their pairing combination is like B-C, D-E & H-L.

Program counter

It is a 16-bit register used to store the memory address location of the next instruction to be executed. Microprocessor increments the program whenever an instruction is being executed, so that the program counter points to the memory address of the next instruction that is going to be executed.

Stack pointer

It is also a 16-bit register works like stack, which is always incremented/ decremented by 2 during push & pop operations.

Temporary register

It is an 8-bit register, which holds the temporary data of arithmetic and logical operations.

Flag register

It is an 8-bit register having five 1-bit flip-flops, which holds either 0 or 1 depending upon the result stored in the accumulator.

These are the set of 5 flip-flops –

- Sign (S)
- Zero (Z)
- Auxiliary Carry (AC)
- Parity (P)
- Carry (C)

Its bit position is shown in the following table –

D7	D6	D5	D4	D3	D2	D1	D0
S	Z		AC		P		CY

Bit Position

Instruction register and decoder

It is an 8-bit register. When an instruction is fetched from memory then it is stored in the Instruction register. Instruction decoder decodes the information present in the Instruction register.

Timing and control unit

It provides timing and control signal to the microprocessor to perform operations. Following are the timing and control signals, which control external and internal circuits –

- Control Signals: READY, RD', WR', ALE
- Status Signals: S0, S1, IO/M'
- DMA Signals: HOLD, HLDA
- RESET Signals: RESET IN, RESET OUT

Interrupt control

As the name suggests it controls the interrupts during a process. When a microprocessor is executing a main program and whenever an interrupt occurs, the microprocessor shifts the control from the main program to process the incoming request. After the request is completed, the control goes back to the main program.

There are 5 interrupt signals in 8085 microprocessor: INTR, RST 7.5, RST 6.5, RST 5.5, TRAP.

Serial Input/output control

It controls the serial data communication by using these two instructions: SID (Serial input data) and SOD (Serial output data).

Address buffer and address-data buffer

The content stored in the stack pointer and program counter is loaded into the address buffer and address-data buffer to communicate with the CPU. The memory and I/O chips are connected to these buses; the CPU can exchange the desired data with the memory and I/O chips.

Address bus and data bus

Data bus carries the data to be stored. It is bidirectional, whereas address bus carries the location to where it should be stored and it is unidirectional. It is used to transfer the data & Address I/O devices.

8085 Architecture:

We have tried to depict the architecture of 8085 with this following image –

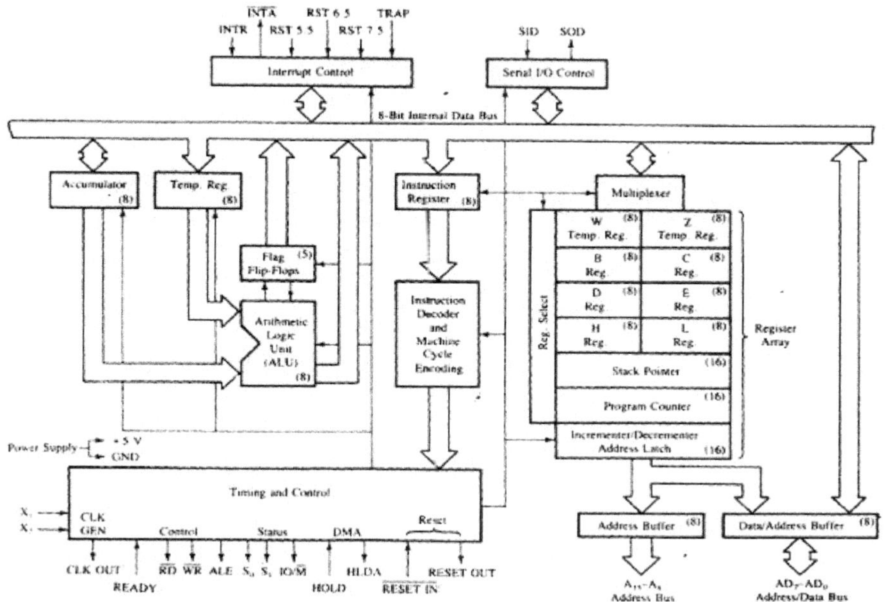

8085 Architecture

FOUR

Microprocessor - 8085 Pin Configuration

The following image depicts the pin diagram of 8085 Microprocessor –

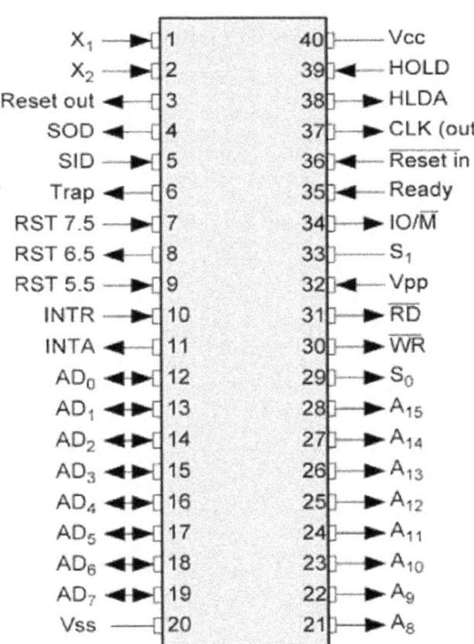

8085-Pin Configuration

The pins of a 8085 microprocessor can be classified into seven groups –

Address bus

A15-A8, it carries the most significant 8-bits of memory/IO address.

Data bus

AD7-AD0, it carries the least significant 8-bit address and data bus.

Control and status signals

These signals are used to identify the nature of operation. There are 3 control signal and 3 status signals.

Three control signals are RD, WR & ALE.

- **RD** – This signal indicates that the selected IO or memory device is to be read and is ready for accepting data available on the data bus.
- **WR** – This signal indicates that the data on the data bus is to be written into a selected memory or IO location.
- **ALE** – It is a positive going pulse generated when a new operation is started by the microprocessor. When the pulse goes high, it indicates address. When the pulse goes down it indicates data.

Three status signals are IO/M, S0 & S1.

- **IO/M**

This signal is used to differentiate between IO and Memory operations, i.e. when it is high indicates IO operation and when it is low then it indicates memory operation.

- **S1 & S0**

These signals are used to identify the type of current operation.

Power supply

There are 2 power supply signals – VCC & VSS. VCC indicates +5v power supply and VSS indicates ground signal.

Clock signals

There are 3 clock signals, i.e. X1, X2, CLK OUT.

- **X1, X2** – A crystal (RC, LC N/W) is connected at these two pins and is used to set frequency of the internal clock generator. This frequency is internally divided by 2.

- **CLK OUT** – This signal is used as the system clock for devices connected with the microprocessor.

Interrupts & externally initiated signals

Interrupts are the signals generated by external devices to request the microprocessor to perform a task. There are 5 interrupt signals, i.e. TRAP, RST 7.5, RST 6.5, RST 5.5, and INTR. We will discuss interrupts in detail in interrupts section.

- INTA – It is an interrupt acknowledgment signal.
- RESET IN – This signal is used to reset the microprocessor by setting the program counter to zero.
- RESET OUT – This signal is used to reset all the connected devices when the microprocessor is reset.
- READY – This signal indicates that the device is ready to send or receive data. If READY is low, then the CPU has to wait for READY to go high.
- HOLD – This signal indicates that another master is requesting the use of the address and data buses.
- HLDA (HOLD Acknowledge) – It indicates that the CPU has received the HOLD request and it will relinquish the bus in the next clock cycle. HLDA is set to low after the HOLD signal is removed.

Serial I/O signals

There are 2 serial signals, i.e. SID and SOD and these signals are used for serial communication.

- SOD (Serial output data line) – The output SOD is set/reset as specified by the SIM instruction.
- SID (Serial input data line) – The data on this line is loaded into accumulator whenever a RIM instruction is executed.

FIVE

MICROPROCESSOR - 8085 ADDRESSING MODES & INTERRUPTS

Now let us discuss the addressing modes in 8085 Microprocessor.

Addressing Modes in 8085:

These are the instructions used to transfer the data from one register to another register, from the memory to the register, and from the register to the memory without any alteration in the content. Addressing modes in 8085 is classified into 5 groups –

- **Immediate addressing mode**

    In this mode, the 8/16-bit data is specified in the instruction itself as one of its operand. For example: MVI K, 20F: means 20F is copied into register K.

- **Register addressing mode**

    In this mode, the data is copied from one register to another. For example: MOV K, B: means data in register B is copied to register K.

- **Direct addressing mode**

In this mode, the data is directly copied from the given address to the register. For example: LDB 5000K: means the data at address 5000K is copied to register B.

- **Indirect addressing mode**

In this mode, the data is transferred from one register to another by using the address pointed by the register. For example: MOV K, B: means data is transferred from the memory address pointed by the register to the register K.

- **Implied addressing mode**

This mode doesn't require any operand; the data is specified by the opcode itself. For example: CMP.

Interrupts in 8085:

Interrupts are the signals generated by the external devices to request the microprocessor to perform a task. There are 5 interrupt signals, i.e. TRAP, RST 7.5, RST 6.5, RST 5.5, and INTR.

Interrupt are classified into following groups based on their parameter –

- **Vector interrupt** – In this type of interrupt, the interrupt address is known to the processor. For example: RST7.5, RST6.5, RST5.5, TRAP.
- **Non-Vector interrupt** – In this type of interrupt, the interrupt address is not known to the processor so, the interrupt address needs to be sent externally by the device to perform interrupts. For example: INTR.
- **Maskable interrupt** – In this type of interrupt, we can disable the interrupt by writing some instructions into the program. For example: RST7.5, RST6.5, RST5.5.
- **Non-Maskable interrupt** – In this type of interrupt, we cannot disable the interrupt by writing some instructions into the program. For example: TRAP.
- **Software interrupt** – In this type of interrupt, the programmer has to add the instructions into the program to execute the interrupt. There are

8 software interrupts in 8085, i.e. RST0, RST1, RST2, RST3, RST4, RST5, RST6, and RST7.

- **Hardware interrupt** – There are 5 interrupt pins in 8085 used as hardware interrupts, i.e. TRAP, RST7.5, RST6.5, RST5.5, INTA.

Note – NTA is not an interrupt, it is used by the microprocessor for sending acknowledgement. TRAP has the highest priority, then RST7.5 and so on.

Interrupt Service Routine (ISR)

A small program or a routine that when executed, services the corresponding interrupting source is called an ISR.

TRAP

It is a non-maskable interrupt, having the highest priority among all interrupts. Bydefault, it is enabled until it gets acknowledged. In case of failure, it executes as ISR and sends the data to backup memory. This interrupt transfers the control to the location 0024H.

RST7.5

It is a maskable interrupt, having the second highest priority among all interrupts. When this interrupt is executed, the processor saves the content of the PC register into the stack and branches to 003CH address.

RST 6.5

It is a maskable interrupt, having the third highest priority among all interrupts. When this interrupt is executed, the processor saves the content of the PC register into the stack and branches to 0034H address.

RST 5.5

It is a maskable interrupt. When this interrupt is executed, the processor saves the content of the PC register into the stack and branches to 002CH address.

INTR

It is a maskable interrupt, having the lowest priority among all interrupts. It can be disabled by resetting the microprocessor.

When INTR signal goes high, the following events can occur –

- The microprocessor checks the status of INTR signal during the execution of each instruction.
- When the INTR signal is high, then the microprocessor completes its current instruction and sends active low interrupt acknowledge signal.

- When instructions are received, then the microprocessor saves the address of the next instruction on stack and executes the received instruction.

SIX

MICROPROCESSOR - 8085 INSTRUCTION SETS

Terms which are used in instruction of 8085 microprocessor:

Opcode: The Opcode is operation codes in the microprocessor which is done addition, multiplication, etc operation.

Operand: The operand contains the data or memory location in the register. If operation worked 1+2 then 1 and 2 are operands.

Mnemonic: The mnemonic in the microprocessor is acronym/ abbreviation, for operation. It is used mnemonics in instruction code to make easy and suitable coding. The mnemonics are R used for the register, A for the accumulator, z for zero flags, add for addition, etc.

Instruction sets are instruction codes to perform some task. It is classified into five categories.

- ***Control Instructions:***

Opcode	Operand	Meaning	Explanation
NOP	None	No operation	No operation is performed, i.e., the instruction is fetched and decoded.
HLT	None	Halt and enter wait state	The CPU finishes executing the current instruction and stops further execution. An interrupt or reset is necessary to exit from the halt state
DI	None	Disable interrupts	The interrupt enable flip-flop is reset and all the interrupts are disabled except TRAP.
EI	None	Enable interrupts	The interrupt enable flip-flop is set and all the interrupts are enabled.
RIM	None	Read interrupt mask	This instruction is used to read the status of interrupts 7.5, 6.5, 5.5 and read serial data input bit
SIM	None	Set interrupt mask	This instruction is used to implement the interrupts 7.5, 6.5, 5.5, and serial data output.

- ***Logical Instructions:***

Logical instructions are the instructions that perform basic logical operations such as AND, OR, etc. In the 8085 microprocessor, the destination operand is always the accumulator. Here logical operation works on a bitwise level.

Opcode	Operand	Meaning	Explanation
CMP	R M	Compare the register or memory with the accumulator	The contents of the operand (register or memory) are M compared with the contents of the accumulator.
CPI	8-bit data	Compare immediate with the accumulator	The second byte data is compared with the contents of the accumulator.
ANA	R M	Logical AND register or memory with the accumulator	The contents of the accumulator are logically AND with M the contents of the register or memory, and the result is placed in the accumulator.
ANI	8-bit data	Logical AND immediate with the accumulator	The contents of the accumulator are logically AND with the 8-bit data and the result is placed in the accumulator.
XRA	R M	Exclusive OR register or memory with the accumulator	The contents of the accumulator are Exclusive OR with M the contents of the register or memory, and the result is placed in the accumulator.
XRI	8-bit data	Exclusive OR immediate with the accumulator	The contents of the accumulator are Exclusive OR with the 8-bit data and the result is placed in the accumulator.
ORA	R M	Logical OR register or memory with the accumulator	The contents of the accumulator are logically OR with M the contents of the register or memory, and result is placed in the accumulator.
ORI	8-bit data	Logical OR immediate with the accumulator	The contents of the accumulator are logically OR with the 8-bit data and the result is placed in the accumulator.
RLC	None	Rotate the accumulator left	Each binary bit of the accumulator is rotated left by one position. Bit D7 is placed in the position of D0 as well as in the Carry flag. CY is modified according to bit D7.
RRC	None	Rotate the accumulator right	Each binary bit of the accumulator is rotated right by one position. Bit D0 is placed in the position of D7 as well as in the Carry flag. CY is modified according to bit D0.
RAL	None	Rotate the accumulator left through carry	Each binary bit of the accumulator is rotated left by one position through the Carry flag. Bit D7 is placed in the Carry flag, and the Carry flag is placed in the least significant position D0. CY is modified according to bit D7.
RAR	None	Rotate the accumulator right through carry	Each binary bit of the accumulator is rotated right by one position through the Carry flag. Bit D0 is placed in the Carry flag, and the Carry flag is placed in the most significant position D7. CY is modified according to bit D0.
CMA	None	Complement accumulator	The contents of the accumulator are complemented. No flags are affected.
CMC	None	Complement carry	The Carry flag is complemented. No other flags are affected.
STC	None	Set Carry	Set Carry

*R=Register & M=Memory

- ***Branching Instructions:***

The three types of branching instructions are:

- Jump (unconditional and conditional)
- Call (unconditional and conditional)
- Return (unconditional and conditional)

Jump Instructions – The jump instruction transfers the program sequence to the memory address given in the operand based on the specified flag. Jump instructions are 2 types: Unconditional Jump Instructions and Conditional Jump Instructions.

(a) Unconditional Jump Instructions: Transfers the program sequence to the described memory address.

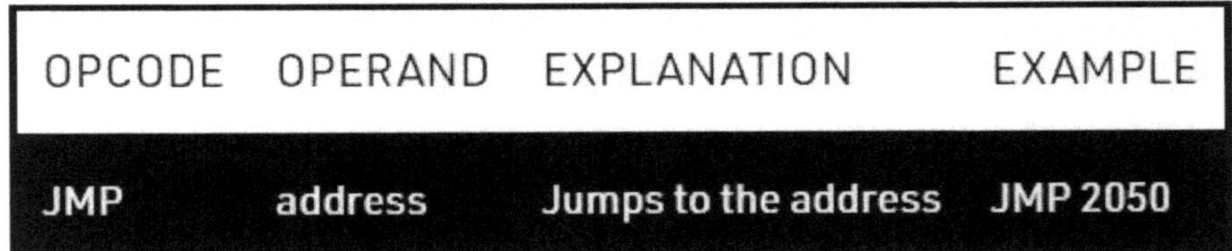

OPCODE	OPERAND	EXPLANATION	EXAMPLE
JMP	address	Jumps to the address	JMP 2050

(b) Conditional Jump Instructions: Transfers the program sequence to the described memory address only if the condition in satisfied.

OPCODE	OPERAND	EXPLANATION	EXAMPLE
JC	address	Jumps to the address if carry flag is 1	JC 2050
JNC	address	Jumps to the address if carry flag is 0	JNC 2050
JZ	address	Jumps to the address if zero flag is 1	JZ 2050
JNZ	address	Jumps to the address if zero flag is 0	JNZ 2050
JPE	address	Jumps to the address if parity flag is 1	JPE 2050
JPO	address	Jumps to the address if parity flag is 0	JPO 2050
JM	address	Jumps to the address if sign flag is 1	JM 2050
JP	address	Jumps to the address if sign flag 0	JP 2050

Call Instructions – The call instruction transfers the program sequence to the memory address given in the operand. Before transferring, the address of the next instruction after CALL is pushed onto the stack. Call instructions are 2 types: Unconditional Call Instructions and Conditional Call Instructions.

(a) Unconditional Call Instructions: It transfers the program sequence to the memory address given in the operand.

OPCODE	OPERAND	EXPLANATION	EXAMPLE
CALL	address	Unconditionally calls	CALL 2050

(b) Conditional Call Instructions: Only if the condition is satisfied, the instructions executes.

OPCODE	OPERAND	EXPLANATION	EXAMPLE
CC	address	Call if carry flag is 1	CC 2050
CNC	address	Call if carry flag is 0	CNC 2050
CZ	address	Calls if zero flag is 1	CZ 2050
CNZ	address	Calls if zero flag is 0	CNZ 2050
CPE	address	Calls if parity flag is 1	CPE 2050
CPO	address	Calls if parity flag is 0	CPO 2050
CM	address	Calls if sign flag is 1	CM 2050
CP	address	Calls if sign flag is 0	CP 2050

Return Instructions – The return instruction transfers the program sequence from the subroutine to the calling program. Return instructions are 2 types: Unconditional Jump Instructions and Conditional Jump Instructions.

(a) Unconditional Return Instruction: The program sequence is transferred unconditionally from the subroutine to the calling program.

OPCODE	OPERAND	EXPLANATION	EXAMPLE
RET	none	Return from the subroutine unconditionally	RET

(b) Conditional Return Instruction: The program sequence is transferred unconditionally from the subroutine to the calling program only is the condition is satisfied.

OPCODE	OPERAND	EXPLANATION	EXAMPLE
RC	none	Return from the subroutine if carry flag is 1	RC
RNC	none	Return from the subroutine if carry flag is 0	RNC
RZ	none	Return from the subroutine if zero flag is 1	RZ
RNZ	none	Return from the subroutine if zero flag is 0	RNZ
RPE	none	Return from the subroutine if parity flag is 1	RPE
RPO	none	Return from the subroutine if parity flag is 0	RPO
RM	none	Returns from the subroutine if sign flag is 1	RM
RP	none	Returns from the subroutine if sign flag is 0	RP

- ***Arithmetic Instructions:***

Arithmetic Instructions are the instructions which perform basic arithmetic operations such as addition, subtraction and a few more. In 8085 microprocessor, the destination operand is generally the accumulator. In 8085 microprocessor, the destination operand is generally the accumulator.

Following is the table showing the list of arithmetic instructions:

Opcode	Operand	Explanation	Example
ADD	R	A = A + R	ADD B
ADD	M	A = A + Mc	ADD 2050
ADI	8-bit data	A = A + 8-bit data	ADI 50
ADC	R	A = A + R + prev. carry	ADC B
ADC	M	A = A + Mc + prev. carry	ADC 2050
ACI	8-bit data	A = A + 8-bit data + prev. carry	ACI 50
SUB	R	A = A - R	SUB B
SUB	M	A = A - Mc	SUB 2050
SUI	8-bit data	A = A - 8-bit data	SUI 50
SBB	R	A = A - R - prev. carry	SBB B
SBB	M	A = A - Mc -prev. carry	SBB 2050
SBI	8-bit data	A = A - 8-bit data - prev. carry	SBI 50
INR	R	R = R + 1	INR B
INR	M	M = Mc + 1	INR 2050
INX	r.p.	r.p. = r.p. + 1	INX H
DCR	R	R = R - 1	DCR B
DCR	M	M = Mc - 1	DCR 2050
DCX	r.p.	r.p. = r.p. - 1	DCX H
DAD	r.p.	HL = HL + r.p.	DAD H

R stands for register
M stands for memory
Mc stands for memory contents
r.p. stands for register pair

- ***Data Transfer Instructions:***

Data transfer instructions are the instructions which transfers data in the microprocessor. They are also called copy instructions.

Following is the table showing the list of logical instructions:

OPCODE	OPERAND	EXPLANATION	EXAMPLE
MOV	Rd, Rs	Rd = Rs	MOV A, B
MOV	Rd, M	Rd = Mc	MOV A, 2050
MOV	M, Rs	M = Rs	MOV 2050, A
MVI	Rd, 8-bit data	Rd = 8-bit data	MVI A, 50
MVI	M, 8-bit data	M = 8-bit data	MVI 2050, 50
LDA	16-bit address	A = contents at address	LDA 2050
STA	16-bit address	contents at address = A	STA 2050
LHLD	16-bit address	directly loads at H & L registers	LHLD 2050
SHLD	16-bit address	directly stores from H & L registers	SHLD 2050
LXI	r.p., 16-bit data	loads the specified register pair with data	LXI H, 3050
LDAX	r.p.	indirectly loads at the accumulator A	LDAX H
STAX	16-bit address	indirectly stores from the accumulator A	STAX 2050
XCHG	none	exchanges H with D, and L with E	XCHG
PUSH	r.p.	pushes r.p. to the stack	PUSH H
POP	r.p.	pops the stack to r.p.	POP H
IN	8-bit port address	inputs contents of the specified port to A	IN 15
OUT	8-bit port address	outputs contents of A to the specified port	OUT 15

R stands for register

M stands for memory

r.p. stands for register pair

RIM instructions in 8085

In 8085 Instruction set, Read Interrupt Mask. It is a 1-Byte multi-purpose instruction. It is used for the following purposes.

- To check whether RST7.5, RST6.5, and RST5.5 are masked or not;
- To check whether interrupts are enabled or not;
- To check whether RST7.5, RST6.5, or RST5.5 interrupts are pending or not;
- To perform serial input of data.

Mnemonics, Operand	Opcode (in HEX)	Bytes
RIM	20	1

To get the status information about the interrupt system, Read Interrupt Mask instruction provides status information about interrupt system and this instruction can be used for serial input of data. Through this RIM instruction, 8085 can know which interrupt is masked or unmasked, etc. The contents of the Accumulator after the execution of the RIM instruction provide this information.

Thus, it is essential to look into the Accumulator contents after the Read Interrupt Mask instruction is executed. The meaning of the various bits of the Accumulator after Read Interrupt Mask is executed is shown in the following figure –

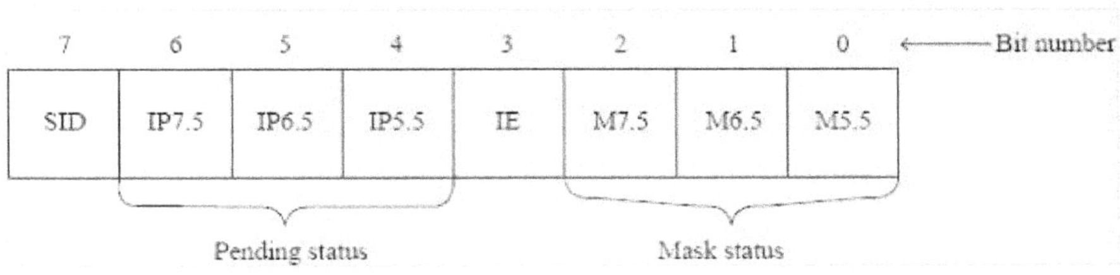

Mask status of interrupts: The LS(Least Significant) 3 bits of the accumulator are used to provide mask status of interrupts. Note that they are not used for masking or unmasking. Masking or unmasking has to be done using the Read Interrupt Mask instruction.

Bit No.	Purpose
Bit 0:	This is mask RST5.5 (M5.5) bit. • If M5.5 = 1, it means that RST5.5 interrupt has been masked. • If M5.5 = 0, RST5.5 interrupt is unmasked.
Bit 1:	This is mask RST6.5 (M6.5) bit. • If M6.5 = 1, it means that RST 6.5 interrupt has been masked. • If M6.5 = 0, RST 6.5 interrupt is unmasked.
Bit 2:	This is mask RST7.5 (M7.5) bit. • If M7.5 = 1, it means that RST 7.5 interrupt has been masked. • If M7.5 = 0, RST7.5 interrupt is unmasked.

Interrupt Enable (IE) status: Bit 3 of the Accumulator provides the status of IE flip-flop after the Read Interrupt Mask instruction is executed.

- If IE = 1, it means that the interrupt system is enabled. This will be the situation if EI instruction is executed sometime prior to the RIM instruction.
- If IE = 0, it means that the interrupt system is disabled. This will be the situation if sometime prior to execution of the RIM instruction, one of the following things have occurred.
- DI instruction was executed
- Intel 8085 has been reset
- Intel 8085 has entered an interrupt service subroutine.

Let us now other status bits in the following table –

Bit No.	Purpose
Bit 4:	This is interrupt pending RST5.5 (IP5.5) bit. ▫ If IP5.5 = 1, it means that RST5.5 interrupt is pending, waiting to be serviced. This will be the situation when RST5.5 interrupt pin is activated, but RST5.5 is masked, or the interrupt system is disabled. ▫ If IP5.5 = 0, the RST5.5interrupt is not pending.
Bit 5:	This is interrupt pending RST6.5 (IP6.5) bit. ▫ If IP6.5 = 1, it means that RST6.5 interrupt is pending, waiting to be serviced. ▫ If IP6.5 = 0, the RST6.5interrupt is not pending.
Bit 6:	This is interrupt pending RST7.5 (IP7.5) bit. ▫ If IP7.5 = 1, it means that RST7.5 interrupt is pending, waiting to be serviced. ▫ If IP7.5 = 0, the RST7.5 interrupt is not pending.

8085 Microprocessor is having one pin labelled Serial Input Data. Which is required for serial data communication. 1-bit of information can be read by the Microprocessor at each single clock pulse. So most significant bit of the Accumulator receives the data present on the SID pin of 8085 when the RIM instruction is executed. In view of this, the meaning of bit 7 of the Accumulator will be as follows, after we execute the RIM instruction.

Bit No.	Purpose
Bit 7:	This is SID bit. After the RIM instruction is executed, the data on the SID pin of 8085 gets loaded into this bit position.

ÞÞÞ

SIM instructions in 8085

In 8085 Instruction set, SIM stands for "SetInterrupt Mask". It is 1-Byte instruction and it is a multi-purpose instruction.

The main uses of SIM instruction are –

- Masking/unmasking of RST7.5, RST6.5, and RST5.5
- Reset to 0 RST7.5 flip-flop
- Perform serial output of data

Mnemonics, Operand	Opcode(in HEX)	Bytes
SIM	30	1

When SIM instruction is executed then the content of theAccumulator decides the action to be taken. So before executing the SIM instruction, it is mandatory to initialize Accumulator with the required value. The meaning and purpose of the various bits of the accumulator when SIM is executed has been depicted below –

7	6	5	4	3	2	1	0	← Bit number
SOD	SOE	X	R7.5	MSE	M7.5	M6.5	M5.5	

Note that except bit 5, which is a don't care bit, the other bits of the Accumulator decide the effect of executing the SIM instruction. Masking of interrupts: Only the LS 4 bits of the accumulator are used for masking or unmasking of interrupts.

Bit No.	Purpose
Bit 3:	This is the Mask Set Enable (MSE) bit. This bit can have two values: 0or 1. ▫ If MSE bit = 0, SIM instruction is not being used for masking or unmasking of interrupts. In such a case, the LS 3bits of the Accumulator are not having any useful information. ▫ If MSE bit = 1, the SIM instruction is used for masking or unmasking of interrupts. Then the LS 3 bits provide information about masking or unmasking of interrupts.
Bit 2:	This is mask RST7.5 (M7.5) bit. Thisbit is meaningful only if MSE bit = 1. If MSE = 1 and M7.5 = 0,RST7.5 is unmasked. If MSE = 1 and M7.5 = 1, RST7.5 is masked.
Bit 1:	This is M6.5 bit, used for masking/unmasking of RST6.5. It is similar to M7.5 bit.
Bit 0:	This is M5.5 bit, used for masking/unmasking of RST5.5. It is similar to M7.5 bit.

It should be noted that RST7.5, RST6.5, and RST5.5 can be masked or unmasked using this SIM instruction. TRAP and INTR cannot be masked or unmasked using SIM. TRAP is not allowed to be masked because it is the highest priority un-maskable interrupt. INTR does do not need the facility of masking because it is the lowest priority interrupt. After reset of 8085 RST7.5, RST6.5, and RST5.5 interrupts will be in masked condition.

Reset RST7.5 flip-flop: Bit 4 (R7.5) of Accumulator is used for resetting to 0 RST7.5 flip-flop output when SIM instruction is executed. If R7.5 = 0, SIM instruction is not being used for resetting of RST7.5 flip-flop. Thus, if R7.5 = 0, there is no change in the RST7.5 flip-flop output. If R7.5 = 1, the RST7.5flip-flop gets cleared. Let us consider the following diagram for the better understanding –

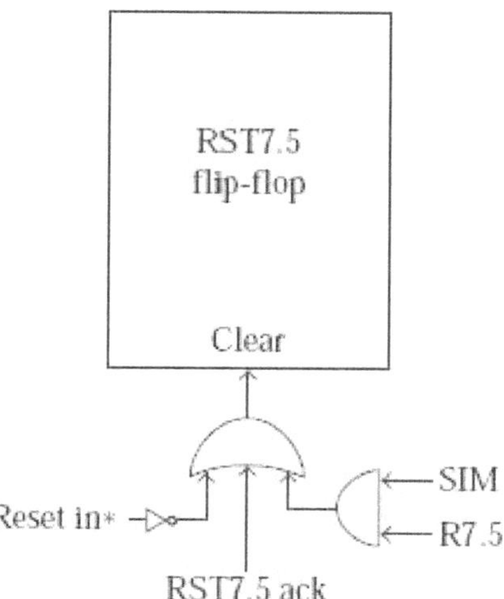

Form the diagram it is clear that SIM signal is activated if and only if, SIM instruction is executed. R7.5 signal is activated when bit 4 (R7.5) of Accumulator = 1. So the RST7.5flip-flop receives logic 1 to its clear input and thus gets cleared when bit 4 of Accumulator = 1 and SIM instruction is executed. Alternatively, RST7.5 flip-flop gets cleared when RST7.5 interrupt is recognized by the 8085 or whenever the 8085 is reset.

In 8085 microprocessor, there is one pin labeled as SOD pin. SOD stands for Serial Output Data. As 8085 is an 8-bit processor, so it generally sends and receives 8-bits of data against each clock pulse. But sometimes parallel communication is not applicable. In those cases, we can select serial communication of8-bit data. That means against each and every clock pulse, 1-bit of information will be transferred. And in this way, it requires 8 clock pulses to transfer 8-bits of data. This is known as serial data communication. Intel 8085 provides SOD (serial output of data) pin and SIM instruction to facilitate serial output of data. The most significant bit of the Accumulator comes out on the SOD pin when the user commands the 8085 to send out the data. The user commands the8085 to send out the MS(Most Significant) bit of Accumulator by making bit 6 of Accumulator as 1 and executing the SIM instruction. Consider the following table –

Bit No.	Purpose
Bit 6:	This is the serial output enables (SOE) bit. If this bit = 0, SIM instruction is not being used for serial output of data. In such a case, the MS bit of Accumulator is not having any useful information. If SOE bit = 1, the SIM instruction is used for serial output of data. Then the MS bit provides the data to be sent out on the SOD pin of 8085.
Bit 7:	This is serial output data (SOD)bit. This bit is meaningful only if SOE bit = 1. If SOE = 1 and SIM instruction is executed, then the SOD bit comes out on the SOD pin of 8085.

SEVEN

Microprocessor - 8085 Assembly Language Programming

Assembly language is specific to a given processor. E.g. assembly language of 8085 is different than that of Motorola 6800 microprocessors. The microprocessor cannot understand a program written in Assembly language. A program known as Assembler is used to convert an Assembly language program to machine language.

1. Six general-purpose Registers
2. Accumulator Register
3. Flag Register
4. Program Counter Register
5. Stack Pointer Register

<u>Six general-purpose registers</u>

– B, C, D, E, H, L

– Can be combined as register pairs to perform 16-bit operations (BC, DE, HL)

<u>Accumulator</u> – identified by name A

– This register is a part of ALU

– 8-bit data storage

– Performs arithmetic and logical operations

– Result of an operation is stored in an accumulator

Flag Register

– This is also a part of ALU

– 8085 has five flags named

• Zero flags (Z)

• Carry flag (CY)

• Sign flag (S)

• Parity flag (P)

• Auxiliary Carry flag (AC) –These flags are five flip-flops in the flag register

–Execution of an arithmetic/logic operation can set or reset these flags

–Condition of flags (set or reset) can be tested through software instructions

–8085 uses these flags in the decision-making process

Program Counter (PC)

– A 16-bit memory pointer register

– Used to sequence execution of a program instructions

– Stores address of a memory location

• where next instruction byte is to be fetched by the 8085

– when 8085 gets busy fetching current instruction from memory

• PC is incremented by one

• PC is now pointing to the address of the next instruction

Stack Pointer Register

– a 16-bit memory pointer register

– Points to a location in Stack memory

– Beginning of the stack is defined by loading a 16-bit address in the stack pointer register.

Instruction Set of 8085

The instruction set, also called ISA (instruction set architecture), is part of a computer that pertains to programming, which is basically machine language. The instruction set provides commands to the processor, to tell it what it needs to do. The instruction set consists of addressing modes, instructions, native data types, registers, memory architecture, interrupt, and exception handling, and external I/O.

There are various popular instruction sets that are used in the industry and are of theoretical importance. Each one has its own usage and advantages. Following are the instruction set architectures:

- Reduced Instruction Set Computer (RISC)

- Complex Instruction Set Computer (CISC)
- Minimal instruction set computers (MISC)
- Very long instruction word (VLIW)
- Explicitly parallel instruction computing (EPIC)
- One instruction set computer (OISC)
- Zero instruction set computer (ZISC)

Reduced Instruction Set Computer (RISC)

Reduced Instruction Set Computer (RISC) is an instruction set architecture (ISA) that has fewer cycles per instruction (CPI) than a complex instruction set computer (CISC). RISC processors are also used in supercomputers such as Summit, which, as of November 2018, is the world's fastest supercomputer as ranked by the TOP500 project.

Complex Instruction Set Computer (CISC)

Complex Instruction Set Computer (CISC) is an instruction set architecture (ISA) that has fewer instructions per program than a Reduced instruction set computer (RISC).

Minimal instruction set computers (MISC)

Minimal instruction set computers (MISC) is a processor architecture with a very small number of basic instruction operations and corresponding opcodes. As a result of this are a smaller instruction set, a smaller and faster instruction set decode unit, and faster operation of individual instructions. The disadvantage is that a smaller instruction set always has more sequential dependencies, reducing instruction-level parallelism.

Very long instruction word (VLIW)

Very long instruction word (VLIW) is an instruction set architecture designed to exploit instruction-level parallelism (ILP). Central processing units (CPU, processor) mostly allow programs to specify instructions to execute in sequence only, a VLIW processor allows programs to explicitly specify instructions to execute in parallel. This design is intended to allow higher performance without the complexity inherent in some other designs.

Explicitly parallel instruction computing (EPIC)

Explicitly parallel instruction computing (EPIC) is an instruction set that permits microprocessors to execute software instructions in parallel by using the compiler, rather than complex on-die circuitry, to control parallel instruction execution. This was intended to allow simple performance scaling without resorting to higher clock frequencies.

One instruction set computer (OISC)

One instruction set computer (OISC) is an abstract machine that uses only one instruction obviating the need for a machine language opcode. OISCs have been recommended as guides in teaching computer architecture and have been used as computational models in structural computing research.

Zero instruction set computer (ZISC)

Zero instruction set computer (ZISC) is a computer architecture based on pattern matching and the absence of (micro-)instructions in the classical sense. These chips are known for being thought of as comparable to the neural networks being marketed for the number of "synapses" and "neurons".

Examples of instruction set

ADD - Add two numbers together.
COMPARE - Compare numbers.
IN - Input information from a device, e.g., keyboard.
JUMP - Jump to designated RAM address.
JUMP IF - Conditional statement that jumps to a designated RAM address.
LOAD - Load information from RAM to the CPU.
OUT - Output information to a device, e.g., monitor.
STORE - Store information to RAM.

Instruction and Data Format

An instruction (instruction format) is a command to the microprocessor to perform a given task on a particular data. Each instruction (instruction format) is of two parts. One is to be performed, called the operation code or opcode and the second one is the data to be operated on, called the operand. Operands or data can be specified in different ways. It may include 8-bit or 16-bit data, an internal register. a memory location, or it or a 16-bit address. In some instructions, the operand is implicit.

Instruction Word Size

The 8085 instruction set is of three groups according to word size:

- One-word or one-byte instructions.
- Two-word or two-byte instructions.
- Three-word or three-byte instructions.

In the 8085 microprocessor, byte and words are synonymous because it is an 8-bit microprocessor. But, instructions are commonly referred to in terms of bytes rather than words.

One-byte instructions

A one-byte instruction includes an opcode and an operand in the same byte. Operand(s) are internal registers and are in the instruction in the codes. If there is no numeral present in the instruction then that instruction will be of one-byte, for example, MOV C, A, RAL, and ADD B, etc. Table M.1 shows examples of one-byte instruction.

Two-byte instructions

In a two-byte instruction, the first byte specifies the operation code and the nd byte specifies the operand. The source operand is a data byte and immediately following the opcode. If an 8-bit numeral is present in the instruction then that instruction will be of two-byte. Here, the numeral may be data or an address. For example, in MVI A, 35H and IN 29H, etc. In a two-byte instruction, the first byte will be the opcode and the second byte will be for the numeral present in the instruction.

Three-byte instructions

In a three-byte instruction, the first byte specifies the opcode, and the following two bytes specify the 16-bit operand. The second byte is the low-order operand and the third byte is the high-order operand. If a 16-bit numeral is present in the instruction then that instruction will be of three-byte. Here, the numeral may be a data or an address, for example, in LXI H,3500H.

8085 program

Problem – Write an assembly language program to add two 8 bit numbers stored at address 2050 and address 2051 in 8085 microprocessor. The starting address of the program is taken as 2000.

Solution:

Algorithm –

1. Load the first number from memory location 2050 to accumulator.
2. Move the content of accumulator to register H.
3. Load the second number from memory location 2051 to accumaltor.
4. Then add the content of register H and accumulator using "ADD" instruction and storing result at 3050

5. The carry generated is recovered using "ADC" command and is stored at memory location 3051.

Program –

Memory Address	Mnemonics	Comment
2000	LDA 2050	A<-[2050]
2003	MOV H, A	H<-A
2004	LDA 2051	A<-[2051]
2007	ADD H	A<-A+H
2008	MOV L, A	L←A
2009	MVI A 00	A←00
200B	ADC A	A←A+A+carry
200C	MOV H, A	H←A
200D	SHLD 3050	H→3051, L→3050
2010	HLT	

Explanation –

1. LDA 2050 moves the contents of 2050 memory location to the accumulator.
2. MOV H, A copies contents of Accumulator to register H to A
3. LDA 2051 moves the contents of 2051 memory location to the accumulator.

4. ADD H adds contents of A (Accumulator) and H register (F9). The result is stored in A itself. For all arithmetic instructions A is by default an operand and A stores the result as well
5. MOV L, A copies contents of A (34) to L
6. MVI A 00 moves immediate data (i.e., 00) to A
7. ADC A adds contents of A(00), contents of register specified (i.e A) and carry (1). As ADC is also an arithmetic operation, A is by default an operand and A stores the result as well
8. MOV H, A copies contents of A (01) to H
9. SHLD 3050 moves the contents of L register (34) in 3050 memory location and contents of H register (01) in 3051 memory location
10. HLT stops executing the program and halts any further execution.

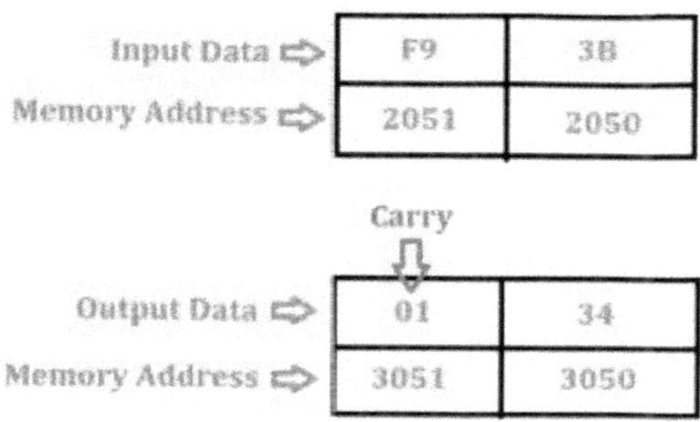

Problem: Write an assembly language program to add two 16 bit numbers by using:

1. 8-bit operation
2. 16-bit operation

Solution:

1. Addition of 16-bit numbers using 8-bit operation:

It is a lengthy method and requires more memory as compared to the 16-bit operation.

Algorithm:

1. Load the lower part of the first number in the B register.
2. Load the lower part of the second number in A (accumulator).
3. Add both the numbers and store.
4. Load the higher part of the first number in the B register.
5. Load the higher part of the second number in A (accumulator).
6. Add both the numbers with carrying from the lower bytes (if any) and store them at the next location.

Program:

MEMORY ADDRESS	MNEMONICS	COMMENTS
2000	LDA 2050	A←2050
2003	MOV B, A	B←A
2004	LDA 2052	A←2052
2007	ADD B	A←A+B
2008	STA 3050	A→3050
200B	LDA 2051	A←2051
200E	MOV B, A	B←A
200F	LDA 2053	A←2053
2012	ADC B	A←A+B+CY
2013	STA 3051	A→3051
2016	HLT	Stops execution

Explanation:

1. LDA 2050 stores the value at 2050 in A (accumulator).
2. MOV B, A stores the value of A into the B register.

3. LDA 2052 stores the value at 2052 in A.
4. ADD B add the contents of B and A and store them in A.
5. STA 3050 stores the result in memory location 3050.
6. LDA 2051 stores the value at 2051 in A.
7. MOV B, A stores the value of A into the B register.
8. LDA 2053 stores the value at 2053 in A.
9. ADC B adds the contents of B, A, and carry from the lower bit addition and store in A.
10. STA 3051 stores the result in memory location 3051.
11. HLT stops execution.

2. Addition of 16 bit numbers using 16-bit operation:

It is a very short method and less memory is also required as compared to 8-bit operations.

Algorithm:

1. Load both the lower and the higher bits of the first number at once.
2. Copy the first number to another registered pair.
3. Load both the lower and the higher bits of second number at once.
4. Add both the register pairs and store the result in a memory location.

Program:

MEMORY ADDRESS	MNEMONICS	COMMENTS
2000	LHLD 2050	H-L ← 2050
2003	XCHG	D ⟷ H & E ⟷ L
2004	LHLD 2052	H-L ← 2052
2007	DAD D	H ← H+D & L ← L+E
2008	SHLD 3050	A → 3050
200B	HLT	Stops execution

Explanation:

1. LHLD 2050 loads the value at 2050 in L register and that in 2051 in the H register (first number)
2. XCHG copies the content of the H to D register and L to E register
3. LHLD 2052 loads the value at 2052 in L register and that in 2053 in the H register (second number)
4. DAD D adds the value of H with D and L with E and stores the result in H and L
5. SHLD 3050 stores the result at memory location 3050
6. HLT stops execution

Problem – Write a program to subtract two 8-bit numbers with or without borrow where first number is at 2500 memory address and second number is at 2501 memory address and store the result into 2502 and borrow into 2503 memory address.

Solution:

Algorithm –

1. Load 00 in a register C (for borrow)
2. Load two 8-bit number from memory into registers
3. Move one number to accumulator
4. Subtract the second number with accumulator
5. If borrow is not equal to 1, go to step 7
6. Increment register for borrow by 1
7. Store accumulator content in memory
8. Move content of register into accumulator
9. Store content of accumulator in other memory location
10. Stop

Program –

Memory	Mnemonics	Operands	Comment
2000	MVI	C, 00	[C] <- 00
2002	LHLD	2500	[H-L] <- [2500]
2005	MOV	A, H	[A] <- [H]
2006	SUB	L	[A] <- [A] – [L]
2007	JNC	200B	Jump If no borrow
200A	INR	C	[C] <- [C] + 1
200B	STA	2502	[A] -> [2502], Result
200E	MOV	A, C	[A] <- [C]
2010	STA	2503	[A] -> [2503], Borrow
2013	HLT		Stop

Explanation –

1. Registers A, H, L, C are used for general purpose:
2. MOV is used to transfer the data from memory to accumulator (1 Byte)
3. LHLD is used to load register pair directly using 16-bit address (3 Byte instruction)
4. MVI is used to move data immediately into any of registers (2 Byte)
5. STA is used to store the content of accumulator into memory(3 Byte instruction)
6. INR is used to increase register by 1 (1 Byte instruction)
7. JNC is used to jump if no borrow (3 Byte instruction)
8. SUB is used to subtract two numbers where one number is in accumulator(1 Byte)
9. HLT is used to halt the program

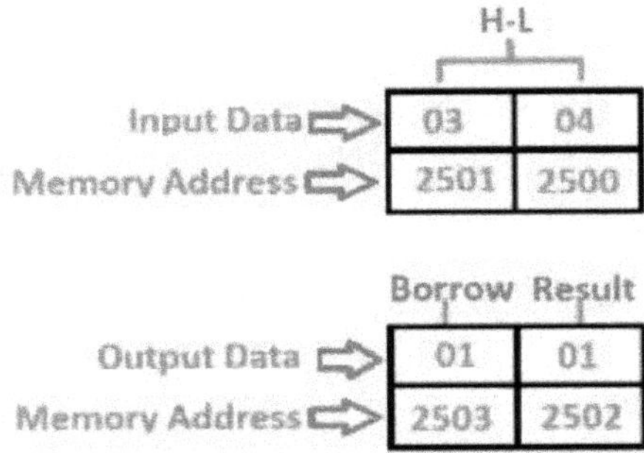

Problem – Multiply two 8 bit numbers stored at address 2050 and 2051. Result is stored at address 3050 and 3051. Starting address of program is taken as 2000.

Solution:

Algorithm –

1. We are taking adding the number 43 seven(7) times in this example.
2. As the multiplication of two 8 bit numbers can be maximum of 16 bits so we need register pair to store the result.

Program –

Memory Address	Mnemonics	Comment
2000	LHLD 2050	H←2051, L←2050
2003	XCHG	H↔D, L↔E
2004	MOV C, D	C←D
2005	MVI D 00	D←00
2007	LXI H 0000	H←00, L←00
200A	DAD D	HL←HL+DE
200B	DCR C	C←C-1
200C	JNZ 200A	If Zero Flag=0, goto 200A
200F	SHLD 3050	H→3051, L→3050
2012	HLT	

Explanation –

1. Registers used: A, H, L, C, D, E
2. LHLD 2050 loads content of 2051 in H and content of 2050 in L
3. XCHG exchanges contents of H with D and contents of L with E
4. MOV C, D copies content of D in C
5. MVI D 00 assigns 00 to D
6. LXI H 0000 assigns 00 to H and 00 to L
7. DAD D adds HL and DE and assigns the result to HL
8. DCR C decrements C by 1
9. JNZ 200A jumps program counter to 200A if zero flag = 0
10. SHLD stores value of H at memory location 3051 and L at 3050
11. HLT stops executing the program and halts any further execution

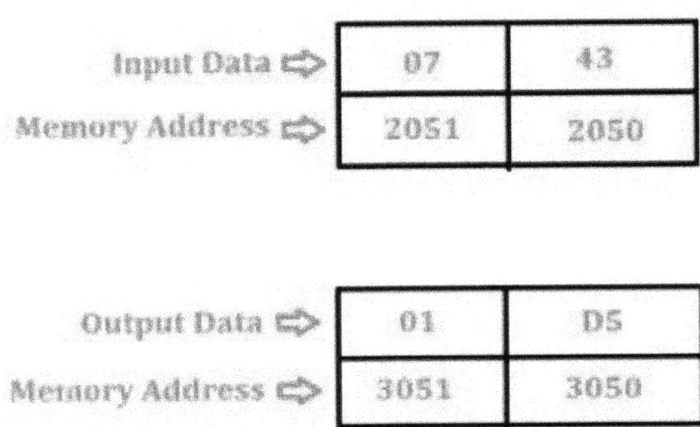

output

Another approach:

- We can do multiplication of two 8-bit numbers without using DAD and XCHG command.

Program-

ADDRESS	MNEMONICS	COMMENT
2000	LXI H, 2050H	
2003	MOV B, M	B←M
2004	INX H	
2005	MOV C, M	C←M
2006	MVI A, 00H	A←00
2008	TOP:ADD B	A<-A+B
2009	DCR C	C←C-1
200A	JNZ TOP	
200D	INX H	
200E	MOV M, A	M←A
200F	HLT	terminate the program

Explanation –Registers A, H, L, C, B are used for general purpose.

1. LXI H, 2050 will load the HL pair register with the address 2050 of memory location.
2. MOV B, M copies the content of memory into register B.
3. INX H will increment the address of HL pair by one and make it 2051H.
4. MOV C,M copies the content of memory into register C.
5. MVI A,00H assign 00 to A.
6. top: ADD B add the content of accumulator with register B and store the result in accumulator.
7. DCR C decrement the register C.
8. JNZ TOP jumps on top till C doesn't becomes 0.
9. INX H will increment the address of HL pair by one and make it 2052H.

10. MOV M,A copies the content of A which is our answer to register M.
11. HLT stops executing the program and halts any further execution.

Problem – Write an assembly language program for calculating the factorial of a number using 8085 microprocessor.

Solution:

In 8085 microprocessor, no direct instruction exists to multiply two numbers, so multiplication is done by repeated addition as 4×3 is equivalent to 4+4+4 (i.e., 3 times).

Load 04H in D register -> Add 04H 3 times -> D register now contains 0CH -> Add 0CH 2 times -> D register now contains 18H -> Add 18H 1 time -> D register now contains 18H -> Output is 18H

Input : 04H

Output : 18H as 04x03x02x01 = 24 in decimal => 18H

Registers B and D after each MULTIPLY function call

B	04H	03H	02H	01H
D (Hexadecimal)	01H	04H	0CH	18H
D (Decimal)	01	04	12	24

Algorithm –

1. Load the data into register B
2. To start multiplication set D to 01H
3. Jump to step 7
4. Decrements B to multiply previous number
5. Jump to step 3 till value of B>0
6. Take memory pointer to next location and store result
7. Load E with contents of B and clear accumulator
8. Repeatedly add contents of D to accumulator E times
9. Store accumulator content to D
10. Go to step 4

Program-

Address	Label	Mnemonic	Comment
2000H	Data		Data Byte
2001H	Result		Result of factorial
2002H		LXI H, 2000H	Load data from memory
2005H		MOV B, M	Load data to B register
2006H		MVI D, 01H	Set D register with 1
2008H	FACTORIAL	CALL MULTIPLY	Subroutine call for multiplication
200BH		DCR B	Decrement B
200CH		JNZ FACTORIAL	Call factorial till B becomes 0
200FH		INX H	Increment memory
2010H		MOV M, D	Store result in memory
2011H		HLT	Halt
2100H	MULTIPLY	MOV E, B	Transfer contents of B to C
2101H		MVI A, 00H	Clear accumulator to store result
2103H	MULTIPLYLOOP	ADD D	Add contents of D to A
2104H		DCR E	Decrement E
2105H		JNZ MULTIPLYLOOP	Repeated addition
2108H		MOV D, A	Transfer contents of A to D
2109H		RET	Return from subroutine

Explanation –

1. First set register B with data.
2. Set register D with data by calling MULTIPLY subroutine one time.
3. Decrement B and add D to itself B times by calling MULTIPLY subroutine as 4*3 is equivalent to 4+4+4 (i.e., 3 times).
4. Repeat the above step till B reaches 0 and then exit the program.
5. The result is obtained in D register which is stored in memory

Data	Result
2000H	2001H
04H	18H

EIGHT
MICROPROCESSOR-SYSTEM

Memory Address Decoding

In Memory Address Decoding, the processor can usually address a memory space that is much larger than the memory space covered by an individual memory chip. In order to splice a memory device into the address space of the processor, decoding is necessary. It refers to the way a computer system decodes the addresses on the address bus to select memory locations in one or more memory or peripheral devices.

- The processor can usually address a memory space that is much larger than the memory space covered by an individual memory chip.
- In order to splice a memory device into the address space of the processor, decoding is necessary.
- For example, the 8088 issues 20-bit addresses for a total of 1MB of memory address space.
- However, the BIOS on a 2716 EPROM has only 2KB of memory and 11 address pins.
- A decoder can be used to decode the additional 9 address pins and allow the EPROM to be placed in any 2KB section of the 1MB address space.

Depending upon the no. of address lines used to generate the chip select signal, the address decoding is classified as:

1. I/O mapped I/O

In this method, a device is identified with an 8-bit address and operated by I/O related functions IN and OUT for that IO/M =1. Since only an 8bit address is used, at most 256 bytes can be identified uniquely. Generally, low order address bits A0-A7 are used and upper bits A8-A15 are considered don't care. Usually, I/O mapped I/O is used to map devices like 8255A, 8251A, etc.

2. Memory-mapped I/O

In this method, a device is identified with a 16-bit address and enabled memory-related functions such as STA, LDA for which IO/M =0, here chip select signal of each device is derived from 16-bit address lines thus total addressing capability is 64K bytes. Usually, memory-mapped I/O is used to map memories like RAM, ROM, etc.

Input/Output Address Decoding

Input/Output Address decoding refers to the way a computer system decodes the addresses on the address bus to select memory locations in one or more memory or peripheral devices. The 68000's 23-bit address bus permits 223 16-bit words to be uniquely addressed. The CPU provides the address of the data desired, but it is the job of the decoding circuitry to locate the selected memory block. To explore the concept of decoding circuitry, we look at various methods used in decoding the addresses. In this discussion, we use SRAM or ROM for the sake of simplicity.

In digital electronics, an address decoder is a binary decoder that has two or more inputs for address bits and one or more outputs for device selection signals. When the address for a particular device appears on the address inputs, the decoder asserts the selection output for that device. A dedicated, single-output may be incorporated into each device on an address bus, or a single may serve multiple devices.

I/O PORT ADDRESS DECODING

- Very similar to memory address decoding, especially for memory-mapped I/O devices.
- The difference between memory decoding and isolated I/O decoding is the number of address pins connected to the decoder.
- In the personal computer system, we always decode all 16 bits of the I/O port address.

Memory Device, Storage, and Classification

Memory storage is just like a human brain. It is used to store data and instruction. Computer memory is the storage space in the computer where data is to be processed and instructions required for processing are stored. The memory is divided into a large number of small parts. Each part is called a cell. Each location or cell has a unique address that varies from zero to memory size minus one. Primary storage, or memory, means the space on your hard drive that is briefly used for working space.

Types of Memory Devices are:

1. RAM
2. ROM
3. Serial Access Memory
4. Direct Access Memory
5. Cache Memory
6. Auxiliary Memory

RAM

A RAM constitutes the internal memory of the CPU for storing data, program, and program results. It is read/write memory. It is called random access memory (RAM). Since access time in RAM is independent of the address to the word that is, each storage location inside the memory is as easy to reach as other locations & takes the same amount of time. We can reach into the memory at random & extremely fast but can also be quite expensive.

RAM is volatile, i.e. data stored in it is lost when we switch off the computer or if there is a power failure. Hence, a backup uninterruptible power system (UPS) is often used with computers. RAM is small, both in terms of its physical size and in the amount of data it can hold.

RAM is of two types:

- Static RAM (SRAM)
- Dynamic RAM (DRAM)

Static RAM (SRAM)

The word static indicates that the memory retains its contents as long as power remains applied. However, data is lost when the power gets down due to its volatile nature. SRAM chips use a matrix of 6-transistors and no capacitors. Transistors do not require power to prevent leakage, so SRAM need not have to be refreshed on a regular basis. Because of the extra space in the matrix, SRAM uses more chips than DRAM for the same amount of storage space, thus making the manufacturing costs higher. Static RAM is used as cache memory needs to be very fast and small.

Dynamic RAM (DRAM)

DRAM, unlike SRAM, must be continually refreshed in order for it to maintain the data. This is done by placing the memory on a refresh circuit that rewrites the data several hundred times per second. The DRAM is used for most system memory because it is cheap and small. All DRAMs are made up of memory cells. These cells are composed of one capacitor and one transistor.

ROM

ROM stands for Read-Only Memory. The memory from which we can only read but cannot write on it. This type of memory is non-volatile. The information is stored permanently in such memories during manufacture.

A ROM, stores such instruction as are required to start a computer when electricity is first turned on, this operation is referred to as bootstrap. ROM chip is not only used in the computer but also in other electronic items like a washing machine and microwave oven.

Following are the various types of ROM –

MROM (Masked ROM)

The very first ROMs were hard-wired devices that contained a pre-programmed set of data or instructions. These kinds of ROMs are known as masked ROMs. It is an inexpensive ROM.

PROM (Programmable Read-Only Memory)

PROM is read-only memory that can be modified only once by a user. The user buys a blank PROM and enters the desired content using a PROM programmer. Inside the PROM chip, there are small fuses that are burnt open during programming. It can be programmed only once and is not erasable.

EPROM (Erasable and Programmable Read-Only Memory)

The EPROM can be erased by exposing it to ultra-violet light for a duration of up to 40 minutes. Usually, an EPROM eraser achieves this function. During programming, an electrical charge is trapped in an insulated gate region. The charge is retained for more than ten years because the charge has no leakage path. For erasing this charge, ultra-violet light is passed through a quartz crystal window (lid). This exposure to ultra-violet light dissipates the charge. During normal use, the quartz lid is sealed with a sticker.

EEPROM (Electrically Erasable and Programmable Read-Only Memory)

The EEPROM is programmed and erased electrically. It can be erased and reprogrammed about ten thousand times. Both erasing and programming take about 4 to 10 ms (millisecond). In EEPROM, any location can be selectively erased and programmed. EEPROMs can be erased one byte at a time, rather than erasing the entire chip. Hence, the process of re-programming is flexible but slow.

Serial Access Memory

Sequential access means the system must search the storage device from the beginning of the memory address until it finds the required piece of data. Memory devise which supports such access is called a Sequential Access Memory or Serial Access Memory. Magnetic tape is an example of serial access memory.

Direct Access Memory

Direct access memory or Random Access Memory, refers to conditions in which a system can go directly to the information that the user wants. Memory devise which supports such access is called a Direct Access Memory. Magnetic disks, optical disks are examples of direct access memory.

Cache Memory

Cache memory is a very high-speed semiconductor memory that can speed up the CPU. It acts as a buffer between the CPU and the main memory. It is used to hold those parts of data and program which are most frequently used by CPU. The parts of data and programs are transferred from disk to cache memory by the operating system, from where the CPU can access them.

Advantages

1. Cache memory is faster than the main memory.
2. It consumes less access time as compared to the main memory.
3. It stores the program that can be executed within a short period of time.
4. It stores data for temporary use.

Disadvantages

1. Cache memory has limited capacity.
2. It is very expensive.

Virtual memory is a technique that allows the execution of processes that are not completely available in memory. The main visible advantage of this scheme is that programs can be larger than physical memory. Virtual memory is the separation of user logical memory from physical memory.

This separation allows an extremely large virtual memory to be provided for programmers when only a smaller physical memory is available. The following are the situations when the entire program is not required to be loaded fully in the main memory.

- User-written error handling routines are used only when an error occurred in the data or computation.
- Certain options and features of a program may be used rarely.
- Many tables are assigned a fixed amount of address space even though only a small amount of the table is actually used.
- The ability to execute a program that is only partially in memory would counter many benefits.
- Less number of I/O would be needed to load or swap each user program into memory.
- A program would no longer be constrained by the amount of physical memory that is available.
- Each user program could take less physical memory, more programs could be run at the same time, with a corresponding increase in CPU utilization and throughput.

Auxiliary Memory

Auxiliary memory is much larger in size than the main memory but is slower. It normally stores system programs, instruction and data files. It is also known as secondary memory. It can also be used as an overflow/virtual memory in case the main memory capacity has been exceeded. Secondary memories cannot be accessed directly by a processor. First, the data/ information of auxiliary memory is transferred to the main memory and then that information can be accessed by the CPU.

Characteristics of Auxiliary Memory are following –

1. Non-volatile memory – Data is not lost when power is cut off.

2. Reusable – The data stays in the secondary storage on a permanent basis until it is not overwritten or deleted by the user.
3. Reliable – Data in secondary storage is safe because of the high physical stability of secondary storage devices.
4. Convenience – With the help of computer software, authorized people can locate and access the data quickly.
5. Capacity – Secondary storage can store large volumes of data in sets of multiple disks.
6. Cost – It is much lesser expensive to store data on a tape or disk than primary memory.

Timing Diagram and machine cycles of 8085 Microprocessor

Timing Diagram: Timing Diagram is a graphical representation. It represents the execution time taken by each instruction in a graphical format. The execution time is represented in T-states.

Instruction Cycle: The time required to execute an instruction is called instruction cycle.

Machine Cycle: The time required to access the memory or input/output devices is called machine cycle.

T-State:

- The machine cycle and instruction cycle takes multiple clock periods.
- A portion of an operation carried out in one system clock period is called as T-state.

Machine cycles of 8085

The 8085 microprocessor has following basic machine cycles. They are

- Opcode fetch cycle (4T)
- Memory read cycle (3 T)
- Memory write cycle (3 T)
- I/O read cycle (3 T)
- I/O write cycle (3 T)

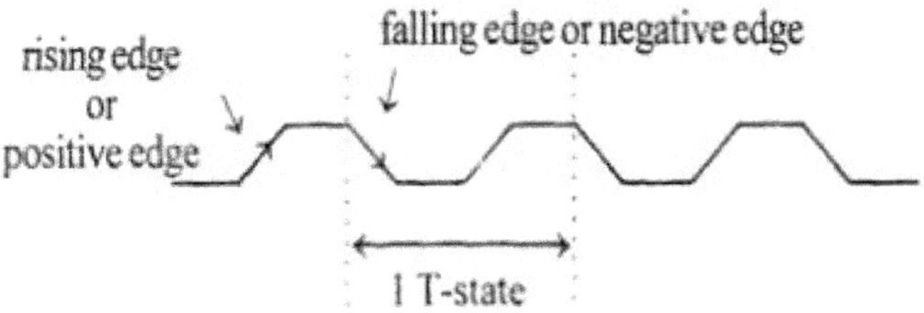

Clock Signal

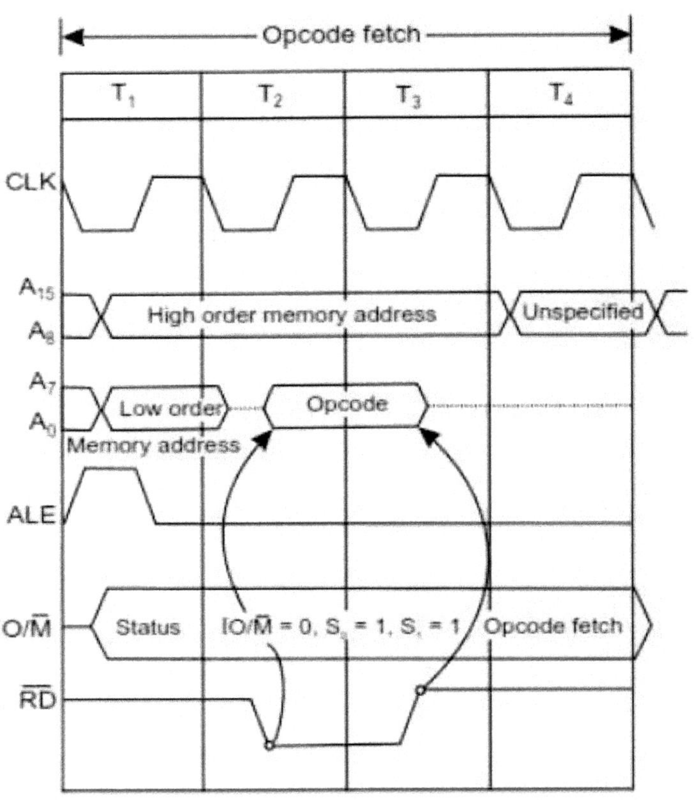

Opcode fetch machine cycle of 8085

- Each instruction of the processor has one byte opcode.
- The opcodes are stored in memory. So, the processor executes the opcode fetch machine cycle to fetch the opcode from memory.
- Hence, every instruction starts with opcode fetch machine cycle.
- The time taken by the processor to execute the opcode fetch cycle is 4T.
- In this time, the first, 3 T-states are used for fetching the opcode from memory and the remaining T-states are used for internal operations by the processor.

Memory Read Machine Cycle of 8085:

- The memory read machine cycle is executed by the processor to read a data byte from memory.
- The processor takes 3T states to execute this cycle.
- The instructions which have more than one byte word size will use the machine cycle after the opcode fetch machine cycle.

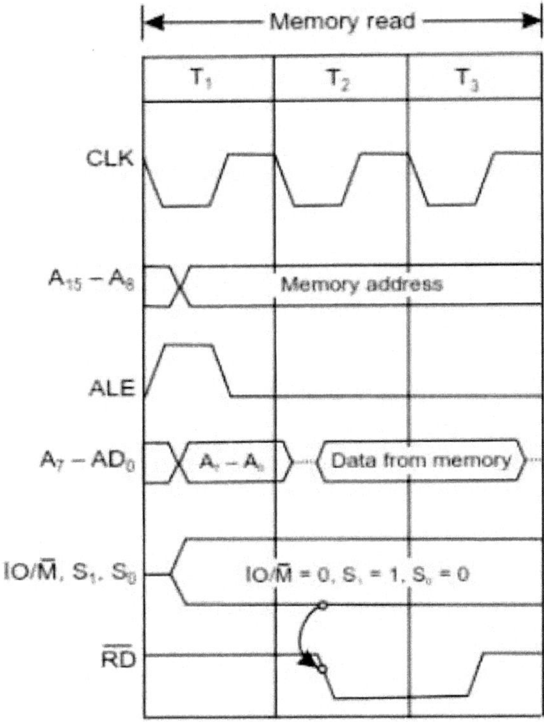

Memory Read Machine Cycle

Memory Write Machine Cycle of 8085:

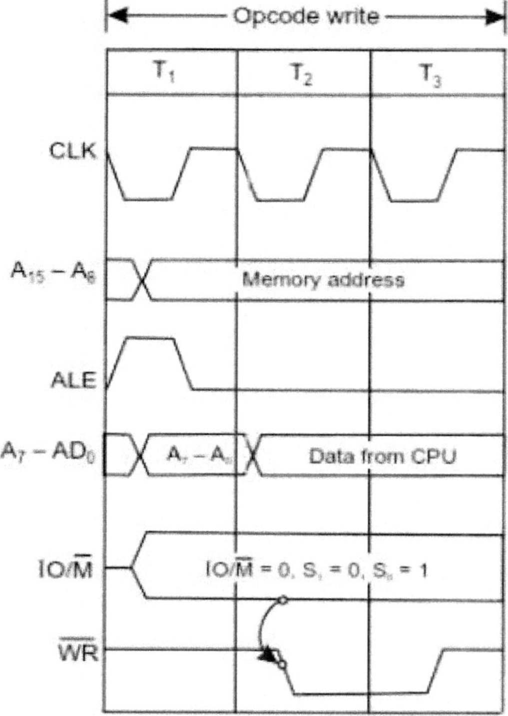

Memory Write Machine Cycle of 8085

- The memory write machine cycle is executed by the processor to write a data byte in a memory location.
- The processor takes, 3T states to execute this machine cycle.

I/O Read Cycle of 8085:

- The I/O Read cycle is executed by the processor to read a data byte from I/O port or from the peripheral, which is I/O, mapped in the system.
- The processor takes 3T states to execute this machine cycle.
- The IN instruction uses this machine cycle during the execution.

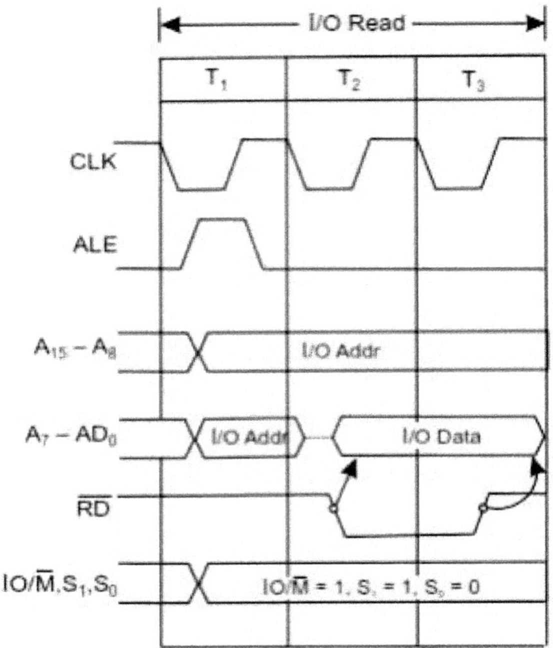

I/O Read Cycle

Timing diagram for STA 526AH:

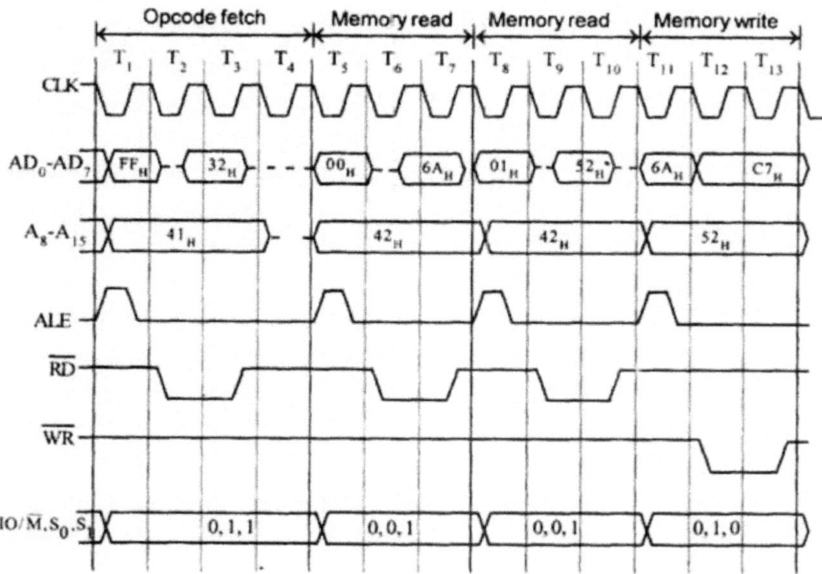

Address	Mnemonics	Opcode
41FF	STA 526AH	32H
4200		6AH
4201		52H

- STA means Store Accumulator -The contents of the accumulator is stored in the specified address (526A).
- The opcode of the STA instruction is said to be 32H. It is fetched from the memory 41FFH (see fig). - OF machine cycle

- Then the lower order memory address is read (6A). - Memory Read Machine Cycle
- Read the higher order memory address (52).- Memory Read Machine Cycle
- The combination of both the addresses are considered and the content from accumulator is written in 526A. - Memory Write Machine Cycle
- Assume the memory address for the instruction and let the content of accumulator is C7H. So, C7H from accumulator is now stored in 526A.

Timing diagram for INR M:

- Fetching the Opcode 34H from the memory 4105H. (OF cycle)
- Let the memory address (M) be 4250H. (MR cycle -To read Memory address and data)
- Let the content of that memory is 12H.
- Increment the memory content from 12H to 13H. (MW machine cycle)

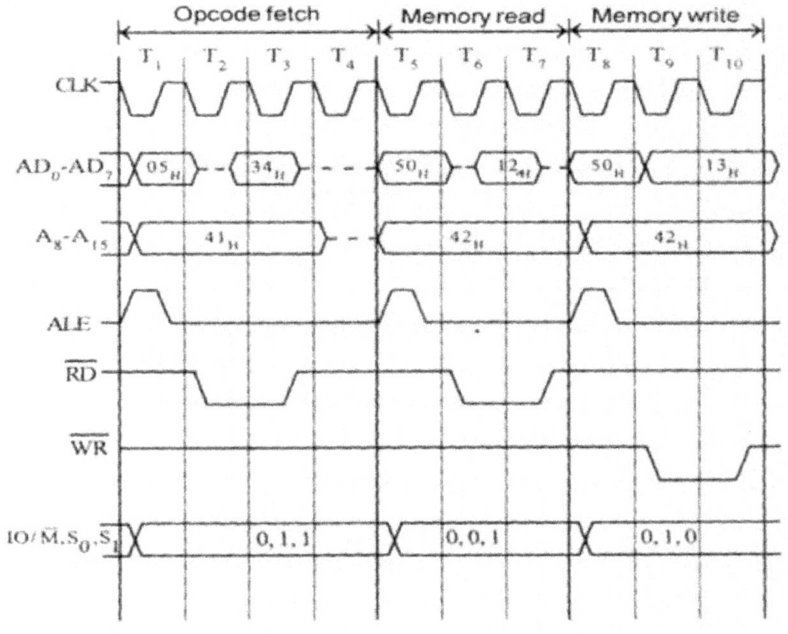

Timing Diagram for INR M

Address	Mnemonics	Opcode
4105	INR M	34_H

Microprocessor Operations

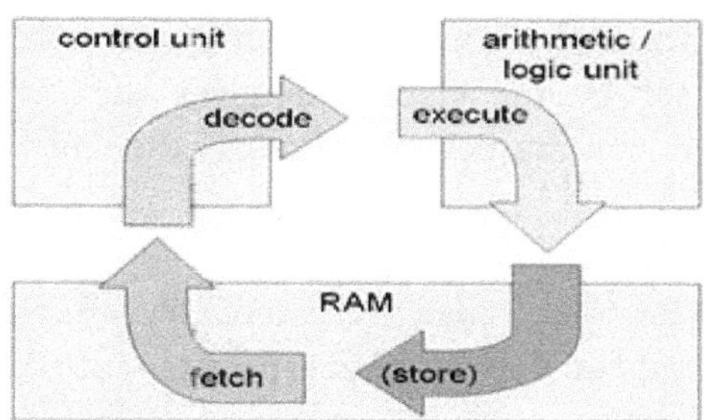

Operations of ALU is arithmetic as well as logical which includes addition, increment, subtraction, decrement, logical operations like AND, OR, Ex-OR, complement, evaluation, left shift or right shift. Both the temporary registers as well as accumulators are utilized for holding the information throughout the operations then the outcome will be stored within the accumulator. The different flags are arranged or rearrange based on the outcome of the operation.

- Flag Registers
- Control and Timing Unit
- Decoder and Instruction Register
- Register Array

- Special Purpose Registers
- Program Counter
- Stack Pointer in 8085
- Increment or Decrement Register
- Address-Buffer & Address-Data-Buffer
- Address Bus and Data Bus
- Timing & Control Unit

Flag Registers

The flag registers of microprocessor 8085 are classified into five types namely sign, zero, auxiliary carry, parity and carry. The positions of bit set aside for these types of flags. After the operation of an ALU, when the result of the most significant bit (D7) is one, then the sign flag will be arranged. When the operation of the ALU outcome is zero then the zero flags will be set. When the outcome is not zero then the zero flags will be reset.

Control and Timing Unit

The control and timing unit coordinates with all the actions of the microprocessor by the clock and gives the control signals which are required for communication among the microprocessor as well as peripherals.

Decoder and Instruction Register

As an order is obtained from memory after that it is located in the instruction register, and encoded & decoded into different device cycles.

Register Array

The general purpose programmable registers are classified into several types apart from the accumulator such as B, C, D, E, H, & L. These are utilized as 8-bit registers otherwise coupled to stock up the 16 bit of data. The permitted couples are BC, DE & HL, and the short term W & Z registers are used in the processor & it cannot be utilized with the developer.

Special Purpose Registers

These registers are classified into four types namely program counter, stack pointer, increment or decrement register, address buffer or data buffer.

Program Counter

This is the first type of special-purpose register and considers that the instruction is being performed by the microprocessor. When the ALU completed performing the instruction, then the microprocessor searches for other instructions to be performed. Thus, there will be a requirement of holding the next instruction address to be performed in order to conserve time. Microprocessor increases the program when an instruction is being performed, therefore that the program counter-position to the next instruction memory address is going to be performed...

Stack Pointer in 8085

The SP or stack pointer is a 16-bit register and functions similar to a stack, which is constantly increased or decreased with two throughout the push and pop processes.

Increment or Decrement Register

The 8-bit register contents or else a memory position can be increased or decreased with one. The 16-bit register is useful for incrementing or decrementing program counters as well as stack pointer register content with one. This operation can be performed on any memory position or any kind of register.

Address-Buffer & Address-Data-Buffer

Address buffer stores the copied information from the memory for the execution. The memory & I/O chips are associated with these buses; then the CPU can replace the preferred data by I/O chips and the memory.

Address Bus and Data Bus

The data bus is useful in carrying the related information that is to be stock up. It is bi-directional, but the address bus indicates the position as to where it must be stored & it is uni-directional, useful for transmitting the information as well as address input/output devices.

Timing & Control Unit

The timing & control unit can be used to supply the signal to the 8085 microprocessor for achieving the particular processes. The timing and control units are used to control the internal as well as external circuits. These are classified into four types namely control units like RD' ALE, READY, WR', status units like S0, S1, and IO/M', DM like HLDA, and HOLD unit, RESET units like RST-IN and RST-OUT.

NINE

Microprocessor-Basic I/O Interfacing

DMA Controlled I/O

The method that is used to transfer information between internal storage and external I/O devices is known as the I/O interface. The CPU is interfaced using special communication links by the peripherals connected to any computer system. These communication links are used to resolve the differences between the CPU and peripheral. There exist special hardware components between the CPU and peripherals to supervise and synchronize all the input and output transfers that are called interface units.

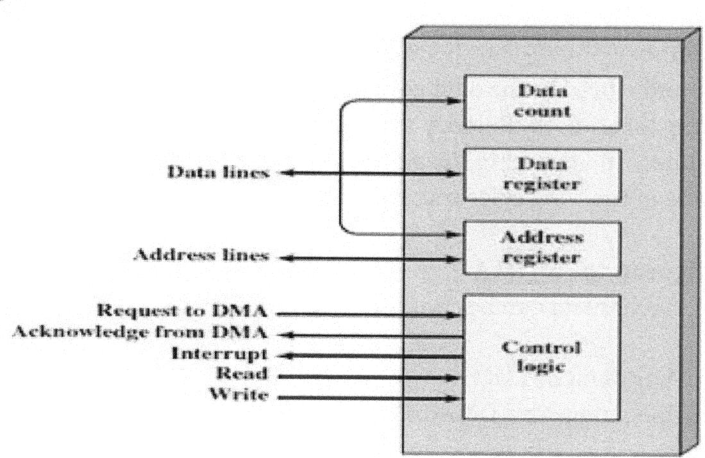

Direct Memory Access (DMA)

Different from Programmed I/O and Interrupt-Driven I/O, Direct Memory Access is a technique for transferring data within the main memory and external device without passing it through the CPU. DMA is a way to improve processor activity and I/O transfer rate by taking over the job of transferring data from the processor and letting the processor do other tasks. This technique overcomes the drawbacks of the other two I/O techniques which are the time-consuming process when issuing the command for data transfer and tie-up the processor in data transfer while the data processing is neglected. It is more efficient to use the DMA method when a large volume of data has to be transferred. For DMA to be implemented, the processor has to share its' system bus with the DMA module. Therefore, the DMA module must use the bus only when the processor does not need it, or it must force the processor to suspend operation temporarily. The latter technique is more common to be used and it is referred to as cycle stealing.

Basic Operation of DMA

When the processor wishes to read or send a block of data, it issues a command to the DMA module by sending some information to the DMA module. The information includes:

- read or write command, sending through reading and write control lines.
- the number of words to be read or written, communicated on the data lines, and stored in the data count register.
- starting location in memory to read from or write to, communicated on data lines, and stored in the address register.
- address of the I/O device involved, communicated on the data lines.

Configurations of DMA

DMA mechanism can be configured in a variety of ways, which are:

- Single-bus detached DMA
- Single-bus integrated DMA-I/O
- I/O bus

Single-bus detached DMA

All modules share the same system bus. The DMA module is acting as a surrogate processor, which uses programmed I/O to exchange data between memory and an I/O module through the DMA module. This configuration is inexpensive but is inefficient. This is because each transfer of a word consumes two bus cycles.

Single-bus integrated DMA

In this configuration, there is a path between the DMA module and one or more I/O modules that do not include the system bus. The DMA logic can be a part of an I/O module or a separate module that controls one or more I/O modules. Therefore, the number of required bus cycles can be cut substantially. The system bus that the DMA module shares with the processor and memory is used by the DMA module only to exchange data with memory. The exchange of data between the DMA and I/O modules takes place off the system bus.

I/O bus

In this configuration, the concept is further improved from the previous configuration, which is single-bus, integrated DMA. I/O modules are connected to the DMA module using an I/O bus. This can reduce the number of I/O interfaces in the DMA module to one and provides for an easily expandable configuration. The system bus that the DMA module shares with the processor and memory is used by the DMA module only to exchange data with memory. The exchange of data between the DMA and I/

O modules takes place off the system bus.

Modes of Parallel transfer

When data is sent using parallel data transmission, multiple data bits are transmitted over multiple channels at the same time. This means that data can be sent much faster than using serial transmission methods.

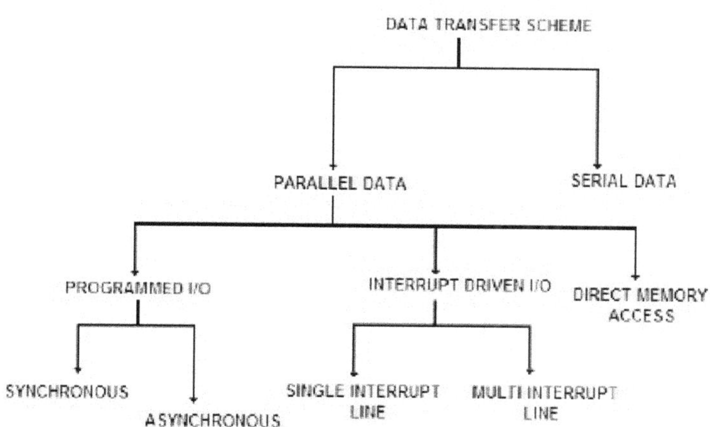

Given that multiple bits are sent over multiple channels at the same time, the order in which a bit string is received can depend on various conditions, such as proximity to the data source, user location, and bandwidth availability. Two examples of parallel interfaces can be seen below. In the first parallel interface, the data is sent and received in the correct order. In the second parallel interface, the data is sent in the correct order, but some bits were received faster than others.

Advantages and Disadvantages of Using Parallel Data Transmission

The main advantages of parallel transmission over serial transmission are:

- It is easier to program;
- and data is sent faster.

Although parallel transmission can transfer data faster, it requires more transmission channels than serial transmission. This means that data bits can be out of sync, depending on transfer distance and how fast each bit loads. A simple example of where this can be seen is with a voice-over IP (VOIP) call when distortion or interference is noticeable. It can also be seen when there is skipping or interference on a video stream.

When is parallel transmission used to send data?

Parallel transmission is used when:

- a large amount of data is being sent;
- the data being sent is time-sensitive;
- and the data needs to be sent quickly.

A scenario where parallel transmission is used to send data is video streaming. When a video is streamed to a viewer, bits need to be received quickly to prevent a video from pausing or buffering. Video streaming also requires the transmission of large volumes of data. The data being sent is also time-sensitive as slow data streams result in poor viewer experience.

Synchronous and Asynchronous Serial Transmission

For Synchronous and Asynchronous Serial Transmission, As we know Serial Transmission data is sent bit by bit, in such a way that each bit follows another. It is of two types namely, Synchronous and Asynchronous Transmission.

Synchronous Transmission

In synchronous transmission, data moves in a completely paired approach, in the form of chunks or frames. Synchronization between the source and target is required so that the source knows where the new byte begins since there are no spaces included between the data.

Synchronous transmission is effective, dependable, and often utilized for transmitting a large amount of data. It offers real-time communication between linked devices. An example of synchronous transmission would be the transfer of a large text file. Before the file is transmitted, it is first dissected into blocks of sentences. The blocks are then transferred over the communication link to the target location.

Characteristics of Synchronous Transmission

- There are no spaces between the characters being sent.
- Timing is provided by modems or other devices at the end of the transmission.
- Special 'syn' characters go before the data being sent.
- The syn characters are included between chunks of data for timing functions.

Examples of Synchronous Transmission

- Chatrooms
- Video conferencing
- Telephonic conversations
- Face-to-face interactions

Asynchronous Transmission

In asynchronous transmission, data moves in a half-paired approach, 1 byte or 1 character at a time. It sends the data in a constant current of bytes. The size of a character transmitted is 8 bits, with a parity bit added both at the beginning and at the end, making it a total of 10 bits. It doesn't need a clock for integration—rather, it utilizes the parity bits to tell the receiver how to translate the data. It is straightforward, quick, cost-effective, and doesn't need 2-way communication to function.

Characteristics of Asynchronous Transmission

Each character is headed by a beginning bit and concluded with one or more end bits.

There may be gaps or spaces in between characters.

Examples of Asynchronous Transmission

- Emails
- Forums
- Letters
- Radios
- Televisions

Synchronous	Asynchronous
• Fast transmission • Needs a common clock signal, or some way of sharing it • May have to wait briefly until data can be sent	• Slower transmission, due to the extra bits and the gaps • Cheap and easy to implement = no clock sharing • Can transmit when ready

- Almost all parallel transmission is synchronous
- Asynchronous transmission is used when data is sent sporadically, e.g. via a mouse or keyboard

Introduction to USART

A USART (Universal Synchronous/Asynchronous Receiver/Transmitter) is a microchip that facilitates communication through a computer's serial port using the RS-232C protocol. USART provides the computer with the interface necessary for communication with modems and other serial devices. However, unlike a UART, a USART offers the option of synchronous mode. In program-to-program communication, the synchronous mode requires that each end of an exchange respond in turn without initiating a new communication. Asynchronous operation means that a process operates independently of other processes.

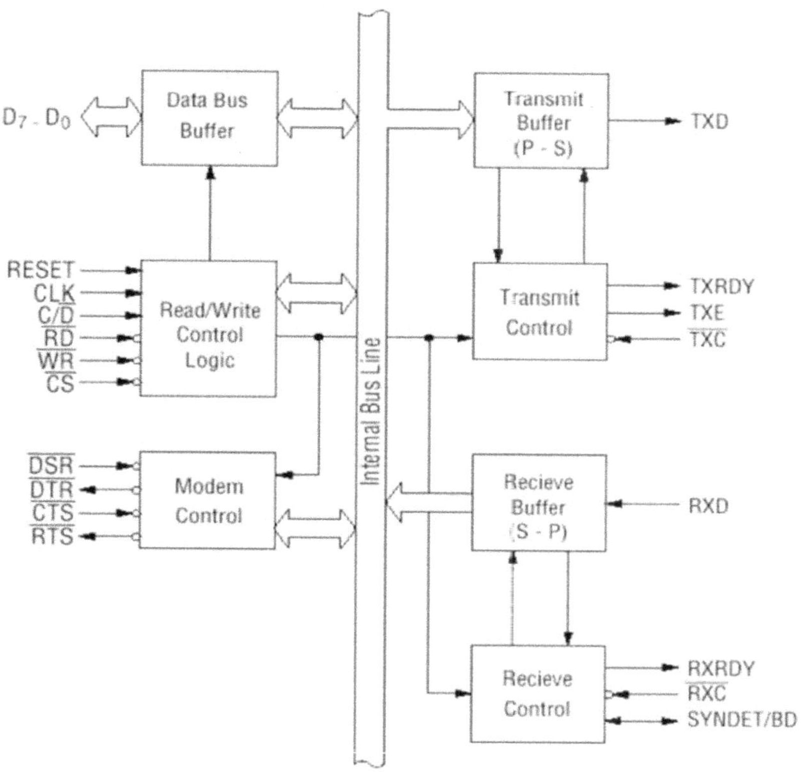

Practical differences between synchronous mode (which is possible only with a USART) and asynchronous mode (which is possible with either a UART or a USART) can be outlined as follows:

- The synchronous mode requires both data and a clock. The asynchronous mode requires only data.
- In synchronous mode, the data is transmitted at a fixed rate. In asynchronous mode, the data does not have to be transmitted at a fixed rate.
- Synchronous data is normally transmitted in the form of blocks, while asynchronous data is normally transmitted one byte at a time.
- Synchronous mode allows for a higher DTR (data transfer rate) than asynchronous mode does if all other factors are held constant.

It contains the following blocks:

1. Data bus buffer –This block helps in interfacing the internal data bus of 8251 to the system data bus. The data transmission is possible between 8251 and CPU by the data bus buffer block.
2. Read/Write control logic –It is a control block for the overall device. It controls the overall work by selecting the operation to be done.
3. Modem control (modulator/demodulator) –A device converts analog signals to digital signals and vice-versa and helps the computers to communicate over telephone lines or cable wires.
4. Transmit buffer –This block is used for parallel to serial converter that receives a parallel byte for conversion into a serial signal and further transmission onto the common channel.
5. Transmit control –This block is used to control the data transmission with the help of the following pins:

- TXRDY: It means the transmitter is ready to transmit data character.
- TXEMPTY: An output signal which indicates that TXEMPTY pin has transmitted all the data characters and transmitter is empty now.
- TXC: An active-low input pin that controls the data transmission rate of transmitted data.

The 8237 DMA Controller

The 8237 DMA Controller stands for 4-channel Direct Memory Access. It is specially designed by Intel for data transfer at the highest speed. Its initial function is to generate a peripheral request which allows the device to transfer the data directly from memory without any interference from the CPU. The 8237 is capable of DMA transfers at rates of up to 1.6 megabytes per second. Each channel is capable of addressing a full 64k-byte section of memory and can transfer up to 64k bytes with single programming. A single 8237 was used as the DMA controller in the original IBM PC and IBM XT. The IBM PC AT added another 8237 in a master-slave configuration, increasing the number of DMA channels from four to seven. Later IBM-compatible personal computers may have chipsets that emulate the functions of the 8237 for backward compatibility.

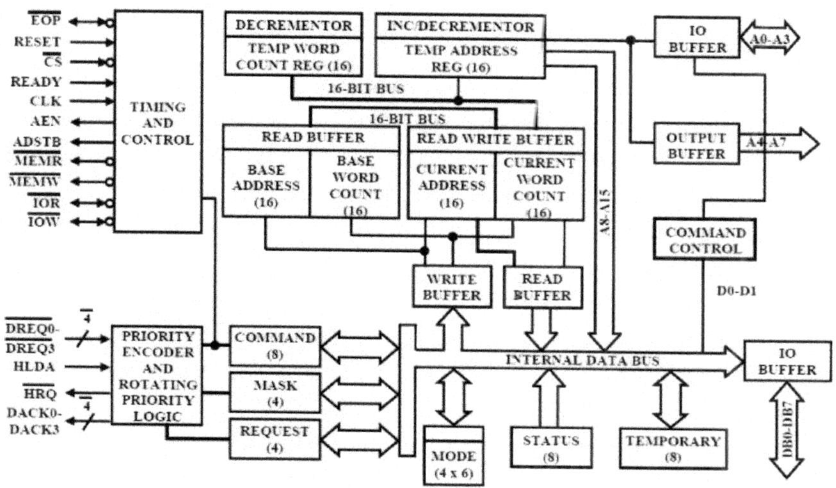

The 8237 operates in four different modes, depending upon the number of bytes transferred per cycle and number of ICs used:

- Single - One DMA cycle, one CPU cycle interleaved until the address counter reaches zero.
- Block - Transfer progresses until the word count reaches zero or the EOP signal goes active.
- Demand - Transfers continue until TC or EOP goes active or DRQ goes inactive. The CPU is permitted to use the bus when no transfer is requested.
- Cascade - Used to cascade additional DMA controllers. DREQ and DACK are matched with HRQ and HLDA from the next chip to establish a priority chain. Actual bus signals are executed by cascaded chips.

The memory-to-memory transfer can be performed. This means data can be transferred from one memory device to another memory device. The channel 0 Current Address register is the source for the data transfer and channel 1 and the transfer terminates when the Current Word Count register becomes 0. Channel 0 is used for DRAM refresh on IBM PC compatibles. In auto initialize mode the address and count values are restored upon reception of an end of process (EOP) signal. This happens without any CPU intervention. It is used to repeat the last transfer.

Single-mode

In a single-mode, only one byte is transferred per request. For every transfer, the counting register is decremented and the address is incremented or decremented depending on programming. When the counting register reaches zero, the terminal count TC signal is sent to the card.

Block transfer mode

The transfer is activated by the DREQ which can be deactivated once acknowledged by DACK. The transfer continues until the end of process EOP (either internal or external) is activated which will trigger terminal count TC to the card. Auto-initialization may be programmed in this mode.

Demand transfer mode

The transfer is activated by DREQ and acknowledged by DACK and continues until either TC, external EOP or DREQ goes inactive. Only TC or external EOP may activate auto-initialization if this is programmed.

Introduction to ISA, PCI, AGP, And USB Interface Standards

Introduction to ISA, PCI, AGP, And USB Interface Standards can explain below.

Introduction to ISA

Short for Industry Standard Architecture, ISA was introduced by IBM and headed by Mark Dean. ISA was originally an 8-bit computer bus that was later expanded to a 16-bit bus in 1984. When this bus was originally released, it was a proprietary bus, which allowed only IBM to create peripherals and the actual interface. However, in the early 1980s, other manufacturers were creating the bus. In 1993, Intel and Microsoft introduced a PnP ISA bus that allowed the computer to automatically detect and set up computer ISA peripherals, such as a modem or sound card. Using the PnP technology, an end-user would have the capability of connecting a device and not having to configure the device using jumpers or dip switches. All modern computers no longer have ISA slots and instead utilizing PCI slots. Below is an example of an ISA expansion card and the ISA slot it connects into the motherboard.

Introduction to PCI

PCI, Stands for "Peripheral Component Interconnect." PCI is a hardware bus used for adding internal components to a desktop computer. For example, a PCI card can be inserted into a PCI slot on a motherboard, providing additional I/O ports on the back of a computer.

Introduction to AGP

Short for an accelerated graphics port, AGP is an advanced port designed for video cards and 3D accelerators. Developed by Intel and introduced in August 1997, AGP introduces a dedicated point-to-point channel that allows the graphics controller direct access to the system memory. Below is an illustration of what the AGP slot may look like on your motherboard.

Introduction to AGP

Accelerated graphics port, AGP is an advanced port designed for video cards and 3D accelerators. Developed by Intel and introduced in August 1997, AGP introduces a dedicated point-to-point channel that allows the graphics controller direct access to the system memory. Below is an illustration of what the AGP slot may look like on your motherboard. The AGP channel is 32-bits wide and runs at 66 MHz, which is a total bandwidth of 266 MBps and much greater than the PCI bandwidth of up to 133 MBps. AGP also supports two optional faster modes, with a throughput of 533 MBps and 1.07 GBps. It also allows 3-D textures to be stored in the main memory rather than video memory. AGP is available in three different versions, the original AGP version mentioned above, AGP 2.0 that was introduced in May 1998, and AGP 3.0 (AGP 8x) were introduced in November 2000. AGP 2.0 added 4x signaling and was capable of operating at 1.5V, and AGP 3.0 was capable of double the transfer speeds.

Introduction to USB

USB is an interface that connects a device to a computer. With this connection, the computer sends or retrieves data from the device. USB gives developers a standard interface to use in many different types of applications. A USB device is easy to connect and use because of a systematic design process. This application note is intended to help make that process simpler.

Basic DMA Operation

Basic DMA Operation refers, Direct Memory Access (DMA) is a method that allows an input/output (I/O) device to send or receive data directly to or from the main memory, bypassing the CPU to speed up memory operations.

The process is managed by a chip known as a DMA controller (DMAC). DMA is a way to improve processor activity and I/O transfer rate by taking over the job of transferring data from the processor and letting the processor do other tasks. This technique overcomes the drawbacks of the other two I/O techniques which are the time-consuming process when issuing commands for data transfer and tie-up the processor in data transfer while the data processing is neglected. It is more efficient to use the DMA method when a large volume of data has to be transferred. For DMA to be implemented, the processor has to share its' system bus with the DMA module. Therefore, the DMA module must use the bus only when the processor does not need it, or it must force the processor to suspend operation temporarily. The latter technique is more common to be used and it is referred to as cycle stealing.

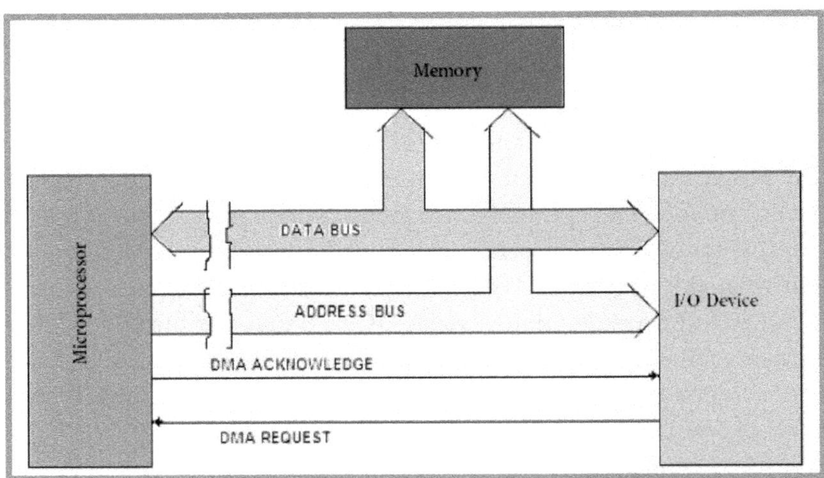

Basic Operation of DMA

When the processor wishes to read or send a block of data, it issues a command to the DMA module by sending some information to the DMA module. The information includes:

- Read or write command, sending through reading and write control lines.
- The number of words to be read or written, communicated on the data lines, and stored in the data count register.

- Starting location in memory to read from or write to, communicated on data lines, and stored in the address register.
- Address of the I/O device involved, communicated on the data lines.

Serial Interfacing

Serial interfacing is a communication interface between two digital systems that transmits data as a series of voltage pulses down a wire. A "1" is represented by a high logical voltage and a "0" is represented by a low logical voltage. Essentially, the serial interface encodes the bits of a binary number by their "temporal" location on a wire rather than their "spatial" location within a set of wires. Encoding data bits by their "spatial" location is referred to as a parallel interface and encoding bits by their "temporal" location is referred to as a serial interface. Figure 3 graphically illustrates the difference between these two communication methods.

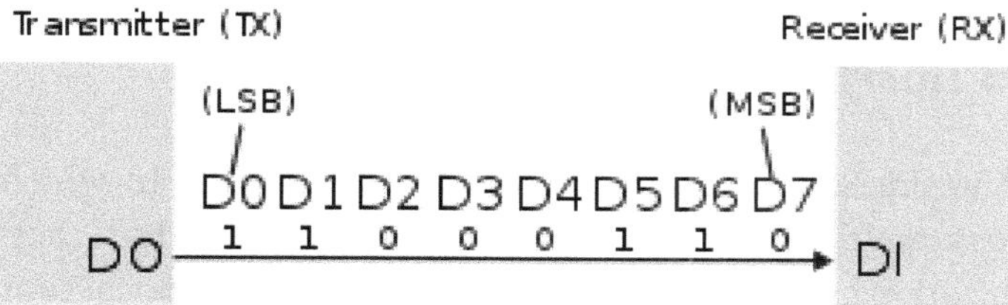

It is the most widely used approach to transfer information between data processing equipment and peripherals. In general, communication means the interchange of information between individuals through written documents, verbal words, audio, and video lessons.

Advantages of Serial Communication over Parallel Communication

There is a misconception that the serial ports/buses are slower than parallel ports/buses as the transmission of data is only a bit per unit of time. Even serial ports/buses may be clocked considerably at a quicker rate than parallel ports/buses and can accomplish a higher speed of data flow. The factors which make Serial Communication better than Parallel Communication are:

- No Clock Required

- Requires Less Space
- No Cross-talks
- Low Cost

No Clock Required

In the case of unclocked and asynchronous type Serial Communication, the problem of clock skew between the lanes/ channels does not exist.

Requires Less Space

The Serial Communication configuration requires less space because the requirement of cable is less in serial connection. The availability of this additional space gives good isolation of the data lanes from the neighboring communication components.

No Cross-talks

There is a minimal presence of conductors in the nearby space. It is, therefore, the chances of cross-talks are rare.

Low Cost

The cost of a serial link is less in comparison to parallel links.

Parallel Interfacing

Parallel interfacing provides a multiline data channel in which bits are sent across multiple conductors simultaneously. The bits must stay in synchronization as they cross the wires, so the parallel interfaces are limited in distance. Parallel interfaces are usually associated with printer connections, but several technologies implement parallel interfaces. A parallel interface refers to a multiline channel, with each line capable of transmitting several bits of data simultaneously. Before USB ports became common, most personal computers (PCs) had at least one parallel interface for connecting a printer using a parallel port. In contrast, a "serial interface" uses a serial port, a single line capable of only transmitting one bit of data at a time; a computer mouse connection is a good example.

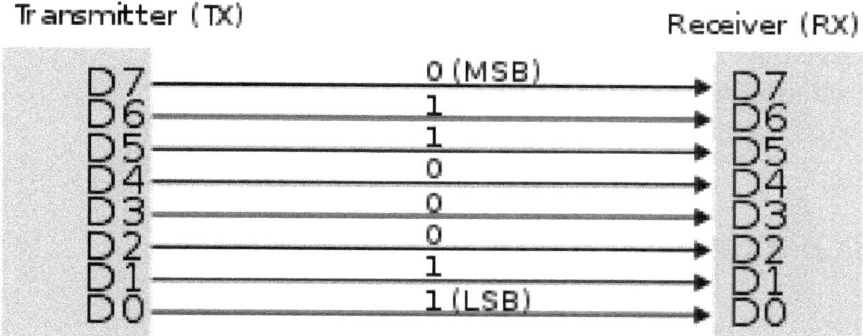

Characteristics

Before the development of high-speed serial communication technologies, the selection of parallel links against serial communication links was decided by the following characteristics:

High-Speed Data transfer

The data exchange speed of a parallel communication data link is equivalent to the multiplication of the number of parallel paths and the number of bits processed at a unit time. Therefore, the more is the parallel path, the higher is the achieved data transfer speed.

Limited Cable Length

As the length of cable increases, so does the amount of metal wires. This increases the chances of Cross-talk. Cross-talk means interference between the cable wires and it leads to the unsuccessful exchange of readable data (garbage value).

Due to this effect, we cannot increase the length of cable beyond a certain safe limit. Owing to this factor, the cable length supported by a parallel link is quite shorter than serial links.

Easy Installation

Parallel data links are relatively easy to be installed as hardware, which in turn makes them a reasonable choice. The configuration of a parallel port in a PC is quite easy as compared to its counterpart 'Serial links'. It is because almost all serial links require its conversion into a parallel form using a Universal asynchronous receiver transmitter to enable it to be connected with a data bus directly.

When to Use Parallel Interfacing

It should be used when:

- Large Data needs to be transferred.
- Data to be sent is time-sensitive.
- Data is required to be transferred quickly or in real-time.

8257 DMA Controller

DMA stands for Direct Memory Access. It is designed by Intel to transfer data at the fastest rate. It allows the device to transfer the data directly to/ from memory without any interference of the CPU.

Using a DMA controller, the device requests the CPU to hold its data, address and control bus, so the device is free to transfer data directly to/ from the memory. The DMA data transfer is initiated only after receiving HLDA signal from the CPU.

How DMA Operations are Performed?

Following is the sequence of operations performed by a DMA –

- Initially, when any device has to send data between the device and the memory, the device has to send DMA request (DRQ) to DMA controller.
- The DMA controller sends Hold request (HRQ) to the CPU and waits for the CPU to assert the HLDA.
- Then the microprocessor tri-states all the data bus, address bus, and control bus. The CPU leaves the control over bus and acknowledges the HOLD request through HLDA signal.
- Now the CPU is in HOLD state and the DMA controller has to manage the operations over buses between the CPU, memory, and I/O devices.

Features of 8257

Here is a list of some of the prominent features of 8257 –

- It has four channels which can be used over four I/O devices.
- Each channel has 16-bit address and 14-bit counter.
- Each channel can transfer data up to 64kb.
- Each channel can be programmed independently.
- Each channel can perform read transfer, write transfer and verify transfer operations.

- It generates MARK signal to the peripheral device that 128 bytes have been transferred.
- It requires a single phase clock.
- Its frequency ranges from 250Hz to 3MHz.
- It operates in 2 modes, i.e., Master mode and Slave mode.

8257 Architecture

The following image shows the architecture of 8257 –

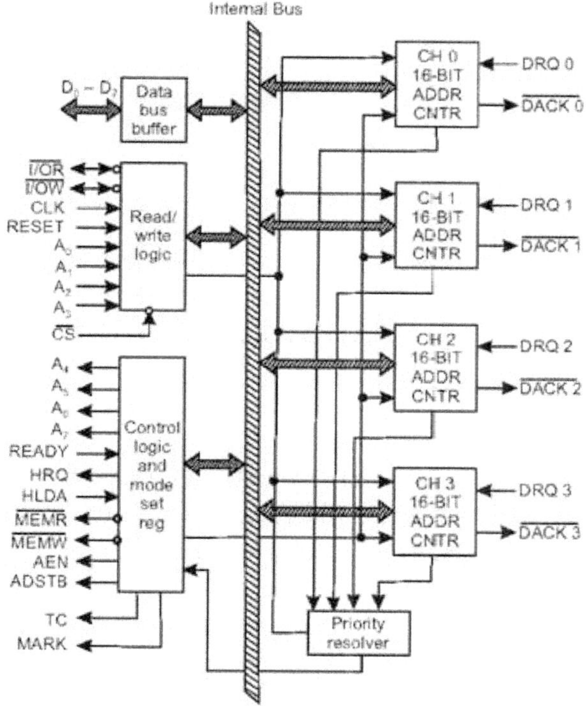

8257 Pin Description

The following image shows the pin diagram of a 8257 DMA controller –

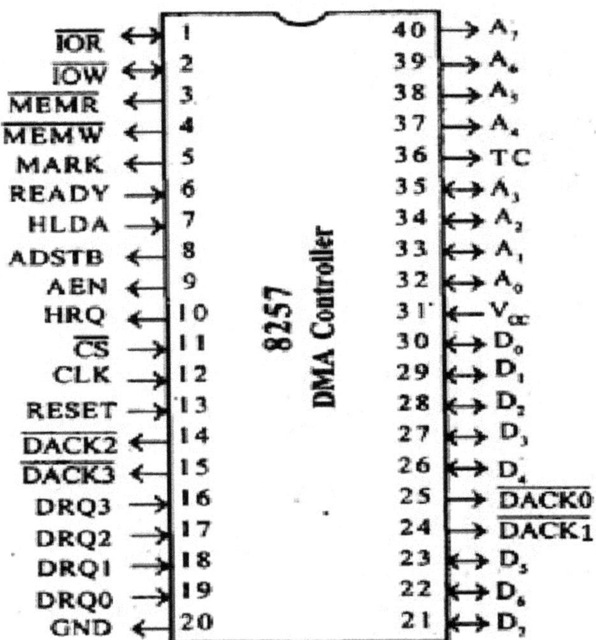

DRQ0–DRQ3

These are the four individual channel DMA request inputs, which are used by the peripheral devices for using DMA services. When the fixed priority mode is selected, then DRQ0 has the highest priority and DRQ3 has the lowest priority among them.

DACKo – DACK3

These are the active-low DMA acknowledge lines, which updates the requesting peripheral about the status of their request by the CPU. These lines can also act as strobe lines for the requesting devices.

Do – D7

These are bidirectional, data lines which are used to interface the system bus with the internal data bus of DMA controller. In the Slave mode, it carries command words to 8257 and status word from 8257. In the master mode, these lines are used to send higher byte of the generated address to the latch. This address is further latched using ADSTB signal.

IOR

It is an active-low bidirectional tri-state input line, which is used by the CPU to read internal registers of 8257 in the Slave mode. In the master mode, it is used to read data from the peripheral devices during a memory write cycle.

IOW

It is an active low bi-direction tri-state line, which is used to load the contents of the data bus to the 8-bit mode register or upper/lower byte of a 16-bit DMA address register or terminal count register. In the master mode, it is used to load the data to the peripheral devices during DMA memory read cycle.

CLK

It is a clock frequency signal which is required for the internal operation of 8257.

RESET

This signal is used to RESET the DMA controller by disabling all the DMA channels.

Ao - A3

These are the four least significant address lines. In the slave mode, they act as an input, which selects one of the registers to be read or written. In the master mode, they are the four least significant memory address output lines generated by 8257.

CS

It is an active-low chip select line. In the Slave mode, it enables the read/write operations to/from 8257. In the master mode, it disables the read/write operations to/from 8257.

A4 - A7

These are the higher nibble of the lower byte address generated by DMA in the master mode.

READY

It is an active-high asynchronous input signal, which makes DMA ready by inserting wait states.

HRQ

This signal is used to receive the hold request signal from the output device. In the slave mode, it is connected with a DRQ input line 8257. In Master mode, it is connected with HOLD input of the CPU.

HLDA

It is the hold acknowledgement signal which indicates the DMA controller that the bus has been granted to the requesting peripheral by the

CPU when it is set to 1.

MEMR

It is the low memory read signal, which is used to read the data from the addressed memory locations during DMA read cycles.

MEMW

It is the active-low three state signal which is used to write the data to the addressed memory location during DMA write operation.

ADST

This signal is used to convert the higher byte of the memory address generated by the DMA controller into the latches.

AEN

This signal is used to disable the address bus/data bus.

TC

It stands for 'Terminal Count', which indicates the present DMA cycle to the present peripheral devices.

MARK

The mark will be activated after each 128 cycles or integral multiples of it from the beginning. It indicates the current DMA cycle is the 128th cycle since the previous MARK output to the selected peripheral device.

Vcc

It is the power signal which is required for the operation of the circuit.

Programmable peripheral interface 8255

PPI 8255 is a general purpose programmable I/O device designed to interface the CPU with its outside world such as ADC, DAC, keyboard etc. We can program it according to the given condition. It can be used with almost any microprocessor.

It consists of three 8-bit bidirectional I/O ports i.e. PORT A, PORT B and PORT C. We can assign different ports as input or output functions.

Block diagram –

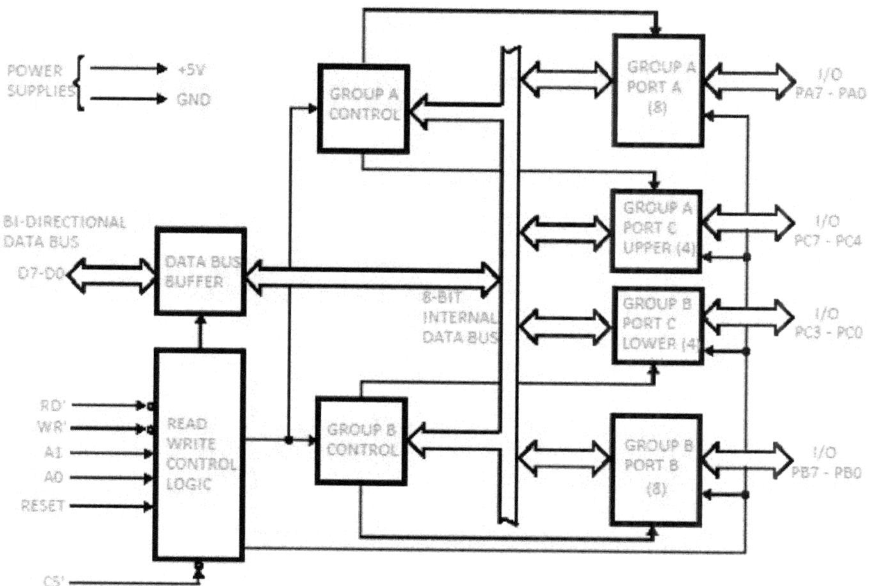

It consists of 40 pins and operates in +5V regulated power supply. Port C is further divided into two 4-bit ports i.e. port C lower and port C upper and port C can work in either BSR (bit set rest) mode or in mode 0 of input-output mode of 8255. Port B can work in either mode 0 or in mode 1 of input-output mode. Port A can work either in mode 0, mode 1 or mode 2 of input-output mode.

It has two control groups, control group A and control group B. Control group A consist of port A and port C upper. Control group B consists of port C lower and port B.

Depending upon the value if CS', A1 and A0 we can select different ports in different modes as input-output function or BSR. This is done by writing a suitable word in control register (control word D0-D7).

CS'	A1	A0	Selection	Address
0	0	0	PORT A	80 H
0	0	1	PORT B	81 H
0	1	0	PORT C	82 H
0	1	1	Control Register	83 H
1	X	X	No Seletion	X

Pin diagram –

		8255		
PA3 ↔	1		40	↔ PA4
PA2 ↔	2		39	↔ PA5
PA1 ↔	3		38	↔ PA6
PA0 ↔	4		37	↔ PA7
RD' →	5		36	← WR'
CS →	6		35	← RESE
GND ←	7		34	↔ D0
VSS →	8		33	↔ D1
A1 →	9		32	↔ D2
A0 ↔	10		31	↔ D3
PC7 ↔	11		30	↔ D4
PC6 ↔	12		29	↔ D5
PC5 ↔	13		28	↔ D6
PC4 ↔	14		27	↔ D7
PC0 ↔	15		26	← VCC
PC2 ↔	16		25	↔ PB7
PC3 ↔	17		24	↔ PB6
PB0 ↔	18		23	↔ PB5
PB1 ↔	19		22	↔ PB4
PB2 ↔	20		21	↔ PB3

- PA0 – PA7 – Pins of port A
- PB0 – PB7 – Pins of port B
- PC0 – PC7 – Pins of port C
- D0 – D7 – Data pins for the transfer of data
- RESET – Reset input
- RD' – Read input
- WR' – Write input
- CS' – Chip select
- A1 and A0 – Address pins

<u>Operating modes –</u>

Bit set reset (BSR) mode –

If MSB of control word (D7) is 0, PPI works in BSR mode. In this mode only port C bits are used for set or reset.

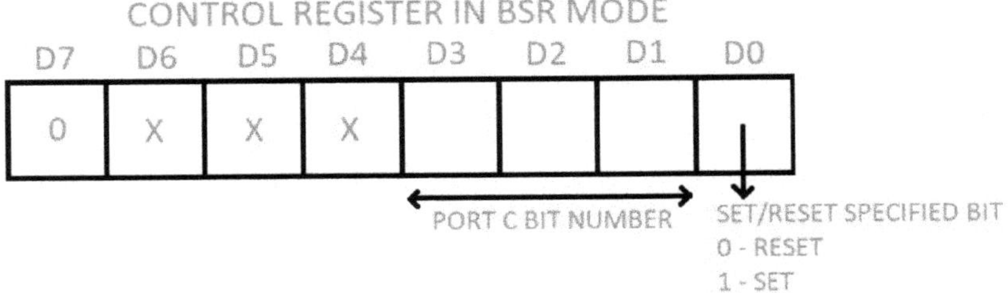

Input-Output mode –

If MSB of control word (D7) is 1, PPI works in input-output mode. This is further divided into three modes:

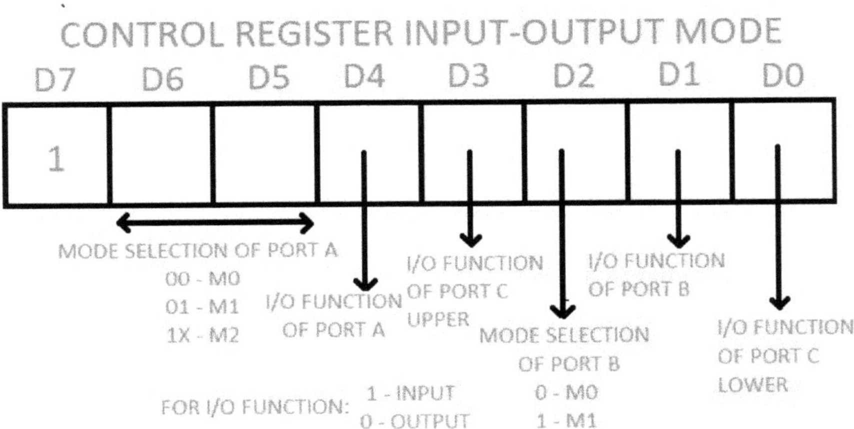

- Mode 0 –In this mode all the three ports (port A, B, C) can work as simple input function or simple output function. In this mode there is no interrupt handling capacity.
- Mode 1 – Handshake I/O mode or strobed I/O mode. In this mode either port A or port B can work as simple input port or simple output port, and port C bits are used for handshake signals before actual data transmission. It has interrupt handling capacity and input and output are latched.

Example: A CPU wants to transfer data to a printer. In this case since speed of processor is very fast as compared to relatively slow printer, so before actual data transfer it will send handshake signals to the printer for synchronization of the speed of the CPU and the peripherals.

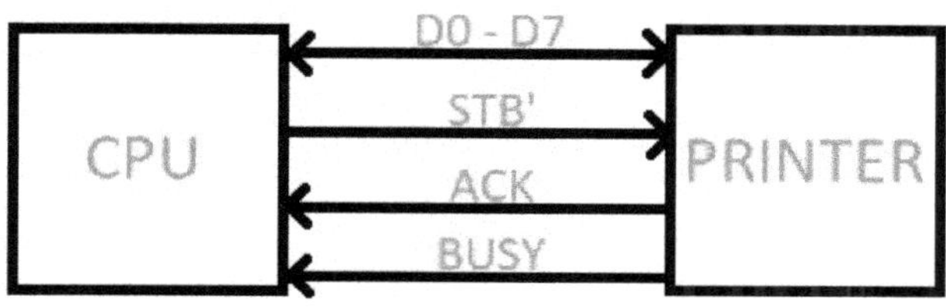

- Mode 2 – Bi-directional data bus mode. In this mode only port A works, and port B can work either in mode 0 or mode 1. 6 bits port C are used as handshake signals. It also has interrupt handling capacity.

8259 PIC Microprocessor

8259 microprocessor is defined as Programmable Interrupt Controller (PIC) microprocessor. There are 5 hardware interrupts and 2 hardware interrupts in 8085 and 8086 respectively. But by connecting 8259 with CPU, we can increase the interrupt handling capability. 8259 combines the multi interrupt input sources into a single interrupt output. Interfacing of single PIC provides 8 interrupts inputs from IR0-IR7.

For example, Interfacing of 8085 and 8259 increases the interrupt handling capability of 8085 microprocessor from 5 to 8 interrupt levels.

Features of 8259 PIC microprocessor –

- Intel 8259 is designed for Intel 8085 and Intel 8086 microprocessor.
- It can be programmed either in level triggered or in edge triggered interrupt level.
- We can masked individual bits of interrupt request register.
- We can increase interrupt handling capability upto 64 interrupt level by cascading further 8259 PIC.
- Clock cycle is not required.

Pin Diagram of 8259 –

$\overline{\text{CS}}$	1		28	Vcc
$\overline{\text{WR}}$	2		27	A0
$\overline{\text{RD}}$	3		26	$\overline{\text{INTA}}$
D7	4		25	IR7
D6	5		24	IR6
D5	6		23	IR5
D4	7	8259	22	IR4
D3	8	PIC	21	IR3
D2	9		20	IR2
D1	10		19	IR1
D0	11		18	IR0
CAS0	12		17	INT
CAS1	13		16	$\overline{\text{SP}}/\overline{\text{EN}}$
Gnd	14		15	CAS2

We can see through pin diagram that there are total 28 pins in 8259 PIC microprocessor where Vcc :5V Power supply and Gnd: ground.

Block Diagram of 8259 PIC microprocessor –

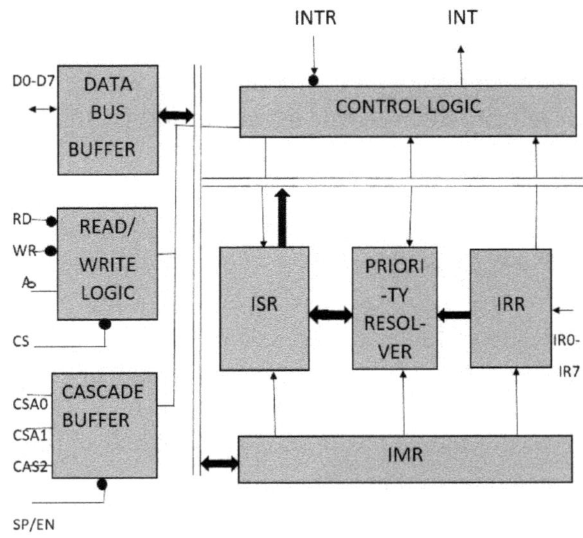

The Block Diagram consists of 8 blocks which are – Data Bus Buffer, Read/Write Logic, Cascade Buffer Comparator, Control Logic, Priority Resolver and 3 registers- ISR, IRR, IMR.

- **Data bus buffer** –This Block is used as a mediator between 8259 and 8085/8086 microprocessor by acting as a buffer. It takes the control word from the 8085 (let say) microprocessor and transfer it to the control logic of 8259 microprocessor. Also, after selection of Interrupt by 8259 microprocessor, it transfer the opcode of the selected Interrupt and address of the Interrupt service sub routine to the other connected microprocessor. The data bus buffer consists of 8 bits represented as D0-D7 in the block diagram. Thus, shows that a maximum of 8 bits data can be transferred at a time.
- **Read/Write logic** –This block works only when the value of pin CS is low (as this pin is active low). This block is responsible for the flow of data depending upon the inputs of RD and WR. These two pins are active low pins used for read and write operations.
- **Control logic** –It is the centre of the microprocessor and controls the functioning of every block. It has pin INTR which is connected with other microprocessor for taking interrupt request and pin INT for giving the output. If 8259 is enabled, and the other microprocessor Interrupt flag is high then this causes the value of the output INT pin high and in this way 8259 responds to the request made by other microprocessor.
- **Interrupt request register (IRR)** –It stores all the interrupt level which are requesting for Interrupt services.
- **Interrupt service register (ISR)** –It stores the interrupt level which are currently being executed.
- **Interrupt mask register (IMR)** –It stores the interrupt level which have to be masked by storing the masking bits of the interrupt level.
- **Priority resolver** –It examines all the three registers and set the priority of interrupts and according to the priority of the interrupts, interrupt with highest priority is set in ISR register. Also, it reset the interrupt level which is already been serviced in IRR.
- **Cascade buffer** –To increase the Interrupt handling capability, we can further cascade more number of pins by using cascade buffer. So, during increment of interrupt capability, CSA lines are used to control multiple

interrupt structure.

SP/EN (Slave program/Enable buffer) pin is when set to high, works in master mode else in slave mode. In Non Buffered mode, SP/EN pin is used to specify whether 8259 work as master or slave and in Buffered mode, SP/EN pin is used as an output to enable data bus.

8254 programmable interval timer

8254 is a device designed to solve the timing control problems in a microprocessor. It has 3 independent counters, each capable of handling clock inputs up to 10 MHz, and size of each counter is 16 bit. It operates in +5V regulated power supply and has 24 pin signals. All modes are software programmable. The 8254 is an advanced version of 8253 which did not offered the feature of read back command.

The basic block diagram of 8254 is:

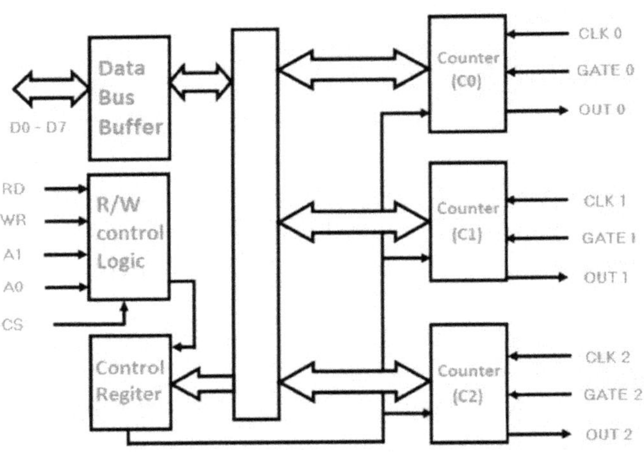

It has 3 counters each with two inputs (Clock and Gate) and one output. Gate is used to enable or disable counting. When any value of count is loaded and value of gate is set(1), after every step value of count is decremented by 1 until it becomes zero.

Depending upon the value of CS, A1, and AC we can determine the addresses of the selected counter.

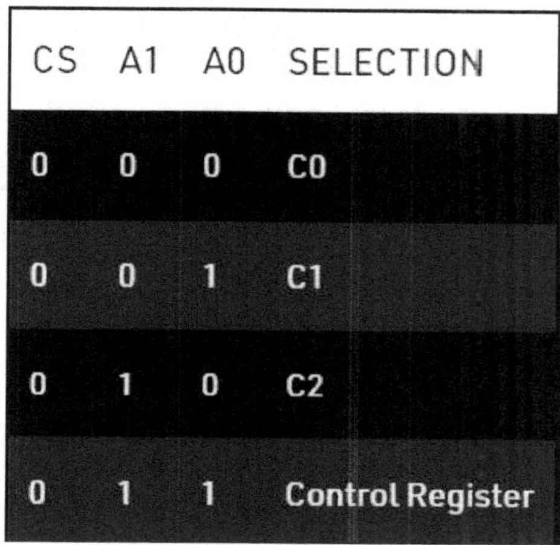

CS	A1	A0	SELECTION
0	0	0	C0
0	0	1	C1
0	1	0	C2
0	1	1	Control Register

Applications –

- To generate an accurate time delay
- As an event counter
- Square wave generator
- Rate generator
- Digital one shot

8279 - Programmable Keyboard

8279 programmable keyboard/display controller is designed by Intel that interfaces a keyboard with the CPU. The keyboard first scans the keyboard and identifies if any key has been pressed. It then sends their relative response of the pressed key to the CPU and vice-a-versa.

How Many Ways the Keyboard is Interfaced with the CPU?

The Keyboard can be interfaced either in the interrupt or the polled mode. In the Interrupt mode, the processor is requested service only if any key is pressed, otherwise the CPU will continue with its main task.

In the Polled mode, the CPU periodically reads an internal flag of 8279 to check whether any key is pressed or not with key pressure.

How Does 8279 Keyboard Work?

The keyboard consists of maximum 64 keys, which are interfaced with the CPU by using the key-codes. These key-codes are de-bounced and stored in an 8-byte FIFORAM, which can be accessed by the CPU. If more than 8 characters are entered in the FIFO, then it means more than eight keys are pressed at a time. This is when the overrun status is set.

If a FIFO contains a valid key entry, then the CPU is interrupted in an interrupt mode else the CPU checks the status in polling to read the entry. Once the CPU reads a key entry, then FIFO is updated, and the key entry is pushed out of the FIFO to generate space for new entries.

Architecture and Description

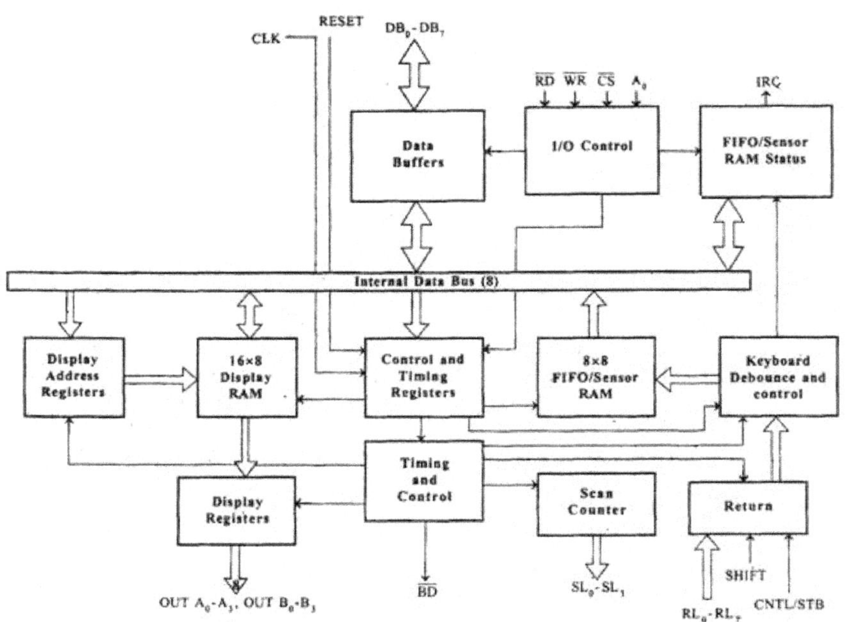

I/O Control and Data Buffer

This unit controls the flow of data through the microprocessor. It is enabled only when D is low. Its data buffer interfaces the external bus of the system with the internal bus of the microprocessor. The pins A0, RD, and WR are used for command, status or data read/write operations.

Control and Timing Register and Timing Control

This unit contains registers to store the keyboard, display modes, and other operations as programmed by the CPU. The timing and control unit handles the timings for the operation of the circuit.

Scan Counter

It has two modes i.e. Encoded mode and Decoded mode. In the encoded mode, the counter provides the binary count that is to be externally decoded to provide the scan lines for the keyboard and display.

In the decoded scan mode, the counter internally decodes the least significant 2 bits and provides a decoded 1 out of 4 scan on SL0-SL3.

Return Buffers, Keyboard Debounce, and Control

This unit first scans the key closure row-wise, if found then the keyboard debounce unit debounces the key entry. In case, the same key is detected, then the code of that key is directly transferred to the sensor RAM along with SHIFT & CONTROL key status.

FIFO/Sensor RAM and Status Logic

This unit acts as 8-byte first-in-first-out (FIFO) RAM where the key code of every pressed key is entered into the RAM as per their sequence. The status logic generates an interrupt request after each FIFO read operation till the FIFO gets empty.

In the scanned sensor matrix mode, this unit acts as sensor RAM where its each row is loaded with the status of their corresponding row of sensors into the matrix. When the sensor changes its state, the IRQ line changes to high and interrupts the CPU.

Display Address Registers and Display RAM

This unit consists of display address registers which holds the addresses of the word currently read/written by the CPU to/from the display RAM.

<u>8279 – Pin Description</u>

The following figure shows the pin diagram of 8279 –

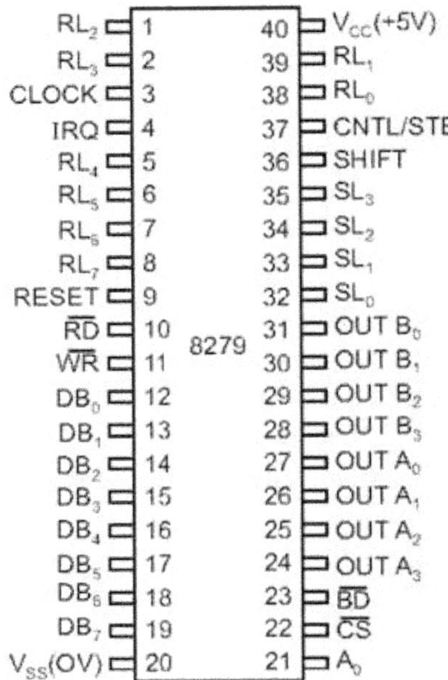

Data Bus Lines, DB0 - DB7

These are 8 bidirectional data bus lines used to transfer the data to/from the CPU.

CLK

The clock input is used to generate internal timings required by the microprocessor.

RESET

As the name suggests this pin is used to reset the microprocessor.

CS Chip Select

When this pin is set to low, it allows read/write operations, else this pin should be set to high.

A0

This pin indicates the transfer of command/status information. When it is low, it indicates the transfer of data.

RD, WR

This Read/Write pin enables the data buffer to send/receive data over the data bus.

IRQ

This interrupt output line goes high when there is data in the FIFO sensor RAM. The interrupt line goes low with each FIFO RAM read operation. However, if the FIFO RAM further contains any key-code entry to be read by the CPU, this pin again goes high to generate an interrupt to the CPU.

Vss, Vcc

These are the ground and power supply lines of the microprocessor.

SL0 – SL3

These are the scan lines used to scan the keyboard matrix and display the digits. These lines can be programmed as encoded or decoded, using the mode control register.

RL0 – RL7

These are the Return Lines which are connected to one terminal of keys, while the other terminal of the keys is connected to the decoded scan lines. These lines are set to 0 when any key is pressed.

SHIFT

The Shift input line status is stored along with every key code in FIFO in the scanned keyboard mode. Till it is pulled low with a key closure, it is pulled up internally to keep it high

CNTL/STB - CONTROL/STROBED I/P Mode

In the keyboard mode, this line is used as a control input and stored in FIFO on a key closure. The line is a strobe line that enters the data into FIFO RAM, in the strobed input mode. It has an internal pull up. The line is pulled down with a key closure.

BD

It stands for blank display. It is used to blank the display during digit switching.

OUTA0 – OUTA3 and OUTB0 – OUTB3

These are the output ports for two 16x4 or one 16x8 internal display refresh registers. The data from these lines is synchronized with the scan lines to scan the display and the keyboard.

Operational Modes of 8279

There are two modes of operation on 8279 – Input Mode and Output Mode.

Input Mode

This mode deals with the input given by the keyboard and this mode is further classified into 3 modes.

- Scanned Keyboard Mode – In this mode, the key matrix can be interfaced using either encoded or decoded scans. In the encoded scan, an 8×8 keyboard or in the decoded scan, a 4×8 keyboard can be interfaced. The code of key pressed with SHIFT and CONTROL status is stored into the FIFO RAM.
- Scanned Sensor Matrix – In this mode, a sensor array can be interfaced with the processor using either encoder or decoder scans. In the encoder scan, 8×8 sensor matrix or with decoder scan 4×8 sensor matrix can be interfaced.
- Strobed Input – In this mode, when the control line is set to 0, the data on the return lines is stored in the FIFO byte by byte.

Output Mode

This mode deals with display-related operations. This mode is further classified into two output modes.

- Display Scan – This mode allows 8/16 character multiplexed displays to be organized as dual 4-bit/single 8-bit display units.
- Display Entry – This mode allows the data to be entered for display either from the right side/left side.

TEN

MICROPROCESSOR - 8086 OVERVIEW

8086 Microprocessor is an enhanced version of 8085Microprocessor that was designed by Intel in 1976. It is a 16-bit Microprocessor having 20 address lines and16 data lines that provides up to 1MB storage. It consists of powerful instruction set, which provides operations like multiplication and division easily.

It supports two modes of operation, i.e. Maximum mode and Minimum mode. Maximum mode is suitable for system having multiple processors and Minimum mode is suitable for system having a single processor.

Features of 8086

- The most prominent features of a 8086 microprocessor are as follows –
- It has an instruction queue, which is capable of storing six instruction bytes from the memory resulting in faster processing.
- It was the first 16-bit processor having 16-bit ALU, 16-bit registers, internal data bus, and 16-bit external data bus resulting in faster processing.

It is available in 3 versions based on the frequency of operation –

- 8086 → 5MHz
- 8086-2 → 8MHz
- 8086-1 → 10 MHz

It uses two stages of pipelining, i.e. Fetch Stage and Execute Stage, which improves performance.

- Fetch stage can prefetch up to 6 bytes of instructions and stores them in the queue.
- Execute stage executes these instructions.

It has 256 vectored interrupts.
It consists of 29,000 transistors.

Comparison between 8085 & 8086 Microprocessor

1. Size – 8085 is 8-bit microprocessor, whereas 8086 is 16-bit microprocessor.
2. Address Bus – 8085 has 16-bit address bus while 8086 has 20-bit address bus.
3. Memory – 8085 can access up to 64Kb, whereas 8086 can access up to 1 Mb of memory.
4. Instruction – 8085 doesn't have an instruction queue, whereas 8086 has an instruction queue.
5. Pipelining – 8085 doesn't support a pipelined architecture while 8086 supports a pipelined architecture.
6. I/O – 8085 can address 2^8 = 256 I/O's, whereas 8086 can access 2^16 = 65,536 I/O's.
7. Cost – The cost of 8085 is low whereas that of 8086 is high.

Architecture of 8086

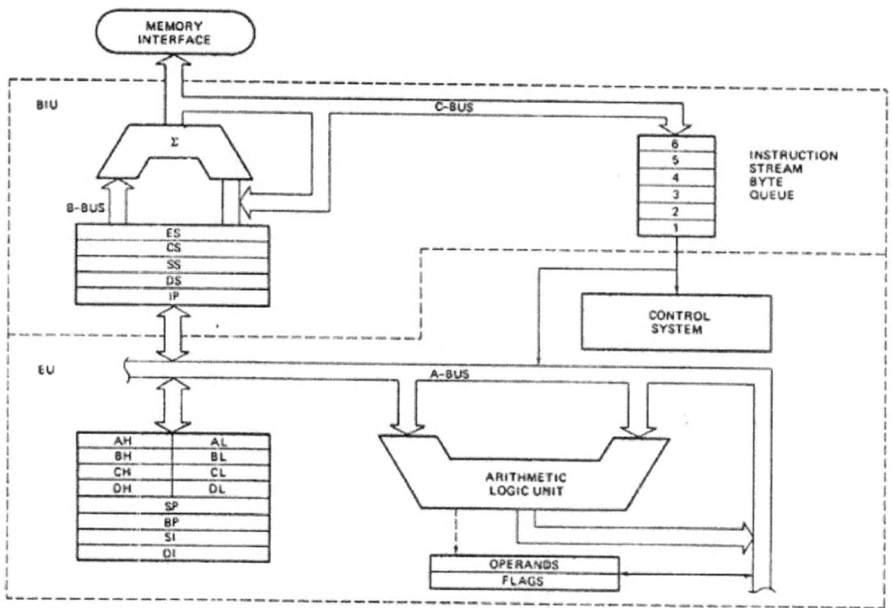

8086 Functional Units

8086 Microprocessor is divided into two functional units, i.e., EU (Execution Unit) and BIU (Bus Interface Unit).

EU (Execution Unit)

Execution unit gives instructions to BIU stating from where to fetch the data and then decode and execute those instructions. Its function is to control operations on data using the instruction decoder & ALU. EU has no direct connection with system buses as shown in the above figure, it performs operations over data through BIU.

Let us now discuss the functional parts of 8086 microprocessors.

ALU

It handles all arithmetic and logical operations, like +, −, ×, /, OR, AND, NOT operations.

Flag Register

It is a 16-bit register that behaves like a flip-flop, i.e. it changes its status according to the result stored in the accumulator. It has 9 flags and they are divided into 2 groups – Conditional Flags and Control Flags.

Conditional Flags

It represents the result of the last arithmetic or logical instruction executed. Following is the list of conditional flags –

- **Carry flag** – This flag indicates an overflow condition for arithmetic operations.
- **Auxiliary flag** – When an operation is performed at ALU, it results in a carry/barrow from lower nibble (i.e. D0 – D3) to upper nibble (i.e. D4 – D7), then this flag is set, i.e. carry given by D3 bit to D4 is AF flag. The processor uses this flag to perform binary to BCD conversion.
- **Parity flag** – This flag is used to indicate the parity of the result, i.e. when the lower order 8-bits of the result contains even number of 1's, then the Parity Flag is set. For odd number of 1's, the Parity Flag is reset.
- **Zero flag** – This flag is set to 1 when the result of arithmetic or logical operation is zero else it is set to 0.
- **Sign flag** – This flag holds the sign of the result, i.e. when the result of the operation is negative, then the sign flag is set to 1 else set to 0.
- **Overflow flag** – This flag represents the result when the system capacity is exceeded.

Control Flags –

Control flags controls the operations of the execution unit. Following is the list of control flags –

- **Trap flag** – It is used for single step control and allows the user to execute one instruction at a time for debugging. If it is set, then the program can be run in a single step mode.
- **Interrupt flag** – It is an interrupt enable/disable flag, i.e. used to allow/prohibit the interruption of a program. It is set to 1 for interrupt enabled condition and set to 0 for interrupt disabled condition.
- **Direction flag** – It is used in string operation. As the name suggests when it is set then string bytes are accessed from the higher memory address to the lower memory address and vice-a-versa.

General purpose register

There are 8 general purpose registers, i.e., AH, AL, BH, BL, CH, CL, DH, and DL. These registers can be used individually to store 8-bit data and can be used in pairs to store 16bit data. The valid register pairs are AH and AL, BH and BL, CH and CL, and DH and DL. It is referred to the AX, BX, CX, and DX respectively.

- **AX register –** It is also known as accumulator register. It is used to store operands for arithmetic operations.
- **BX register –** It is used as a base register. It is used to store the starting base address of the memory area within the data segment.
- **CX register –** It is referred to as counter. It is used in loop instruction to store the loop counter.
- **DX register –** This register is used to hold I/O port address for I/O instruction.

Stack pointer register

It is a 16-bit register, which holds the address from the start of the segment to the memory location, where a word was most recently stored on the stack.

BIU (Bus Interface Unit)

BIU takes care of all data and addresses transfers on the buses for the EU like sending addresses, fetching instructions from the memory, reading data from the ports and the memory as well as writing data to the ports and the memory. EU has no direction connection with System Buses so this is possible with the BIU. EU and BIU are connected with the Internal Bus.

It has the following functional parts –

- **Instruction queue –** BIU contains the instruction queue. BIU gets upto 6 bytes of next instructions and stores them in the instruction queue. When EU executes instructions and is ready for its next instruction, then it simply reads the instruction from this instruction queue resulting in increased execution speed.
- Fetching the next instruction while the current instruction executes is called pipelining.
- **Segment register –** BIU has 4 segment buses, i.e. CS, DS, SS& ES. It holds the addresses of instructions and data in memory, which are used by the processor to access memory locations. It also contains 1 pointer register IP, which holds the address of the next instruction to executed by the EU.

1. **CS –** It stands for Code Segment. It is used for addressing a memory location in the code segment of the memory, where the executable program is stored.
2. **DS –** It stands for Data Segment. It consists of data used by the program andis accessed in the data segment by an offset address or the content of other register that holds the offset address.
3. **SS –** It stands for Stack Segment. It handles memory to store data and addresses during execution.
4. **ES –** It stands for Extra Segment. ES is additional data segment, which is used by the string to hold the extra destination data.

- **Instruction pointer –** It is a 16-bit register used to hold the address of the next instruction to be executed.

ELEVEN

Microprocessor - 8086 Pin Configuration

8086 was the first 16-bit microprocessor available in 40-pin DIP (Dual Inline Package) chip. Let us now discuss in detail the pin configuration of a 8086 Microprocessor.

8086 Pin Diagram

Here is the pin diagram of 8086 microprocessor –

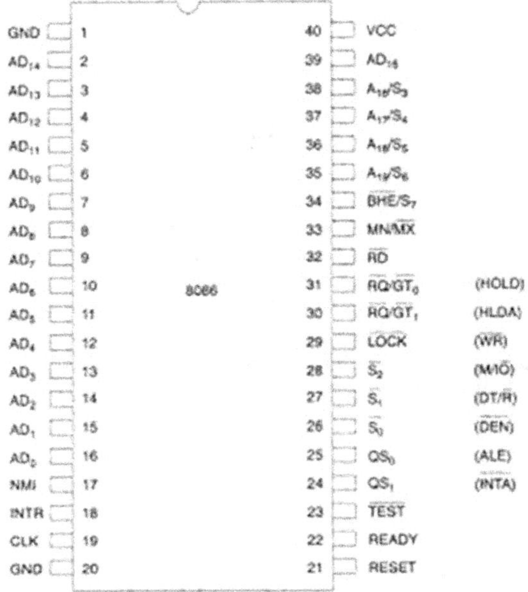

Let us now discuss the signals in detail –

- **Power supply and frequency signals**: It uses 5V DC supply at VCC pin 40, and uses ground at VSS pin 1 and 20 for its operation.
- **Clock signal:** Clock signal is provided through Pin-19. It provides timing to the processor for operations. Its frequency is different for different versions, i.e. 5MHz, 8MHz and 10MHz.
- **Address/data bus:** AD0-AD15. These are 16 address/data bus. AD0-AD7 carries low order byte data and AD8AD15 carries higher order byte data. During the first clock cycle, it carries 16-bit address and after that it carries 16-bit data.
- **Address/status bus:** A16-A19/S3-S6. These are the 4 address/status buses. During the first clock cycle, it carries 4-bit address and later it carries status signals.
- **S7/BHE:** BHE stands for Bus High Enable. It is available at pin 34 and used to indicate the transfer of data using data bus D8-D15. This signal is low during the first clock cycle, thereafter it is active.

- **Read:** It is available at pin 32 and is used to read signal for Read operation.
- **Ready:** It is available at pin 22. It is an acknowledgement signal from I/O devices that data is transferred. It is an active high signal. When it is high, it indicates that the device is ready to transfer data. When it is low, it indicates wait state.
- **RESET:** It is available at pin 21 and is used to restart the execution. It causes the processor to immediately terminate its present activity. This signal is active high for the first 4 clock cycles to RESET the microprocessor.
- **INTR:** It is available at pin 18. It is an interrupt request signal, which is sampled during the last clock cycle of each instruction to determine if the processor considered this as an interrupt or not.
- **NMI:** It stands for non-maskable interrupt and is available at pin 17. It is an edge triggered input, which causes an interrupt request to the microprocessor.
- **TEST:** This signal is like wait state and is available at pin 23. When this signal is high, then the processor has to wait for IDLE state, else the execution continues.
- **MN/MX:** It stands for Minimum/Maximum and is available at pin 33. It indicates what mode the processor is to operate in; when it is high, it works in the minimum mode and vice-aversa.
- **INTA:** It is an interrupt acknowledgement signal and id available at pin 24. When the microprocessor receives this signal, it acknowledges the interrupt.
- **ALE:** It stands for address enable latch and is available at pin 25. A positive pulse is generated each time the processor begins any operation. This signal indicates the availability of a valid address on the address/data lines.
- **DEN:** It stands for Data Enable and is available at pin 26. It is used to enable Transreceiver 8286. The transreceiver is a device used to separate data from the address/data bus.
- **DT/R:** It stands for Data Transmit/Receive signal and is available at pin 27. It decides the direction of data flow through the transreceiver. When it is high, data is transmitted out and vice-a-versa.
- **M/IO:** This signal is used to distinguish between memory and I/O operations. When it is high, it indicates I/O operation and when it is low indicates the memory operation. It is available at pin 28.

- **WR:** It stands for write signal and is available at pin 29. It is used to write the data into the memory or the output device depending on the status of M/IO signal.
- **HLDA:** It stands for Hold Acknowledgement signal and is available at pin 30. This signal acknowledges the HOLD signal.
- **HOLD:** This signal indicates to the processor that external devices are requesting to access the address/data buses. It is available at pin 31.
- **QS1 and QS0:** These are queue status signals and are available at pin 24 and 25. These signals provide the status of instruction queue.

QS_0	QS_1	Status
0	0	No operation
0	1	First byte of opcode from the queue
1	0	Empty the queue
1	1	Subsequent byte from the queue

- **S0, S1, S2:** These are the status signals that provide the status of operation, which is used by the Bus Controller 8288 to generate memory & I/O control signals. These are available at pin 26, 27, and 28.

S_2	S_1	S_0	Status
0	0	0	Interrupt acknowledgement
0	0	1	I/O Read
0	1	0	I/O Write
0	1	1	Halt
1	0	0	Opcode fetch
1	0	1	Memory read
1	1	0	Memory write
1	1	1	Passive

- **LOCK:** When this signal is active, it indicates to the other processors not to ask the CPU to leave the system bus. It is activated using the LOCK prefix on any instruction and is available at pin 29.
- **RQ/GT1 and RQ/GT0:** These are the Request/Grant signals used by the other processors requesting the CPU to release the system bus. When the signal is received by CPU, then it sends acknowledgment. RQ/GT0 has a higher priority than RQ/GT1.

TWELVE

MICROPROCESSOR - 8086 INSTRUCTION SETS

The 8086 microprocessor supports 8 types of instructions –

1. Data Transfer Instructions
2. Arithmetic Instructions
3. Bit Manipulation Instructions
4. String Instructions
5. Program Execution Transfer Instructions (Branch & Loop Instructions)
6. Processor Control Instructions
7. Iteration Control Instructions
8. Interrupt Instructions

Let us now discuss these instruction sets in detail.

Data Transfer Instructions

These instructions are used to transfer the data from the source operand to the destination operand. Following are the list of instructions under this group –

Instruction to transfer a word

- **MOV –** Used to copy the byte or word from the provided source to the provided destination.
- **PPUSH –** Used to put a word at the top of the stack.

- **POP** – Used to get a word from the top of the stack to the provided location.
- **PUSHA** – Used to put all the registers into the stack.
- **POPA** – Used to get words from the stack to all registers.
- **XCHG** – Used to exchange the data from two locations.
- **XLAT** – Used to translate a byte in AL using a table in the memory.

Instructions for input and output port transfer

- **IN** – Used to read a byte or word from the provided port to the accumulator.
- **OUT** – Used to send out a byte or word from the accumulator to the provided port.

Instructions to transfer the address

- **LEA** – Used to load the address of operand into the provided register.
- **LDS** – Used to load DS register and other provided register from the memory
- **LES** – Used to load ES register and other provided register from the memory.

Instructions to transfer flag registers

- **LAHF** – Used to load AH with the low byte of the flag register.
- **SAHF** – Used to store AH register to low byte of the flag register.
- **PUSHF** – Used to copy the flag register at the top of the stack.
- **POPF** – Used to copy a word at the top of the stack to the flag register.

Arithmetic Instructions

These instructions are used to perform arithmetic operations like addition, subtraction, multiplication, division, etc.

Following is the list of instructions under this group –

Instructions to perform addition

- **ADD** – Used to add the provided byte to byte/word to word.
- **ADC** – Used to add with carry.
- **INC** – Used to increment the provided byte/word by 1.

- **AAA** – Used to adjust ASCII after addition.
- **DAA** – Used to adjust the decimal after the addition/subtraction operation.

Instructions to perform subtraction

- **SUB** – Used to subtract the byte from byte/word from word.
- **SBB** – Used to perform subtraction with borrow.
- **DEC** – Used to decrement the provided byte/word by 1.
- **NPG** – Used to negate each bit of the provided byte/word and add 1/2's complement.
- **CMP** – Used to compare 2 provided byte/word.
- **AAS** – Used to adjust ASCII codes after subtraction.
- **DAS** – Used to adjust decimal after subtraction.

Instruction to perform multiplication

- **MUL** – Used to multiply unsigned byte by byte/word by word.
- **IMUL** – Used to multiply signed byte by byte/word by word.
- **AAM** – Used to adjust ASCII codes after multiplication.

Instructions to perform division

- **DIV** – Used to divide the unsigned word by byte or unsigned double word by word.
- **IDIV** – Used to divide the signed word by byte or signed double word by word.
- **AAD** – Used to adjust ASCII codes after division.
- **CBW** – Used to fill the upper byte of the word with the copies of sign bit of the lower byte.
- **CWD** – Used to fill the upper word of the double word with the sign bit of the lower word.

Bit Manipulation Instructions

These instructions are used to perform operations where data bits are involved, i.e. operations like logical, shift, etc.

Following is the list of instructions under this group –

Instructions to perform logical operation

- **NOT –** Used to invert each bit of a byte or word.
- **AND –** Used for adding each bit in a byte/word with the corresponding bit in another byte/word.
- **OR –** Used to multiply each bit in a byte/word with the corresponding bit in another byte/word.
- **XOR –** Used to perform Exclusive-OR operation over each bit in a byte/word with the corresponding bit in another byte/word.
- **TEST –** Used to add operands to update flags, without affecting operands.

Instructions to perform shift operations

- **SHL/SAL –** Used to shift bits of a byte/word towards left and put zero(S) in LSBs.
- **SHR –** Used to shift bits of a byte/word towards the right and put zero(S) in MSBs.
- **SAR –** Used to shift bits of a byte/word towards the right and copy the old MSB into the new MSB.

Instructions to perform rotate operations

- **ROL –** Used to rotate bits of byte/word towards the left, i.e. MSB to LSB and to Carry Flag [CF].
- **ROR –** Used to rotate bits of byte/word towards the right, i.e. LSB to MSB and to Carry Flag [CF].
- **RCR –** Used to rotate bits of byte/word towards the right, i.e. LSB to CF and CF to MSB.
- **RCL –** Used to rotate bits of byte/word towards the left, i.e. MSB to CF and CF to LSB.

String Instructions

String is a group of bytes/words and their memory is always allocated in a sequential order.

Following is the list of instructions under this group –

- **REP –** Used to repeat the given instruction till CX ≠ 0.
- **REPE/REPZ –** Used to repeat the given instruction until CX = 0 or zero flag ZF = 1.

- **REPNE/REPNZ** – Used to repeat the given instruction until CX = 0 or zero flag ZF = 1.
- **MOVS/MOVSB/MOVSW** – Used to move the byte/word from one string to another.
- **COMS/COMPSB/COMPSW** – Used to compare two string bytes/words.
- **INS/INSB/INSW** – Used as an input string/byte/word from the I/O port to the provided memory location.
- **OUTS/OUTSB/OUTSW** – Used as an output string/byte/word from the provided memory location to the I/O port.
- **SCAS/SCASB/SCASW** – Used to scan a string and compare its byte with a byte in AL or string word with a word in AX.
- **LODS/LODSB/LODSW** – Used to store the string byte into AL or string word into AX.

Program Execution Transfer Instructions (Branch and Loop Instructions)

These instructions are used to transfer/branch the instructions during an execution. It includes the following instructions –

Instructions to transfer the instruction during an execution without any condition –

- **CALL** – Used to call a procedure and save their return address to the stack.
- **RET** – Used to return from the procedure to the main program.
- **JMP** – Used to jump to the provided address to proceed to the next instruction.

Instructions to transfer the instruction during an execution with some conditions –

- **JA/JNBE** – Used to jump if above/not below/equal instruction satisfies.
- **JAE/JNB** – Used to jump if above/not below instruction satisfies.
- **JBE/JNA** – Used to jump if below/equal/ not above instruction satisfies.
- **JC** – Used to jump if carry flag CF = 1
- **JE/JZ** – Used to jump if equal/zero flag ZF = 1
- **JG/JNLE** – Used to jump if greater/not less than/equal instruction satisfies.
- **JGE/JNL** – Used to jump if greater than/equal/not less than instruction satisfies.

- **JL/JNGE –** Used to jump if less than/not greater than/equal instruction satisfies.
- **JLE/JNG –** Used to jump if less than/equal/if not greater than instruction satisfies.
- **JNC –** Used to jump if no carry flag (CF = 0)
- **JNE/JNZ –** Used to jump if not equal/zero flag ZF = 0
- **JNO –** Used to jump if no overflow flag OF = 0
- **JNP/JPO –** Used to jump if not parity/parity odd PF = 0
- **JNS –** Used to jump if not sign SF = 0
- **JO –** Used to jump if overflow flag OF = 1
- **JP/JPE –** Used to jump if parity/parity even PF = 1
- **JS –** Used to jump if sign flag SF = 1

Processor Control Instructions

These instructions are used to control the processor action by setting/resetting the flag values.

Following are the instructions under this group –

- **STC –** Used to set carry flag CF to 1
- **CLC –** Used to clear/reset carry flag CF to 0
- **CMC –** Used to put complement at the state of carry flag CF.
- **STD –** Used to set the direction flag DF to 1
- **CLD –** Used to clear/reset the direction flag DF to 0
- **STI –** Used to set the interrupt enable flag to 1, i.e., enable INTR input.
- **CLI –** Used to clear the interrupt enable flag to 0, i.e., disable INTR input.

Iteration Control Instructions

These instructions are used to execute the given instructions for number of times. Following is the list of instructions under this group –

- **LOOP –** Used to loop a group of instructions until the condition satisfies, i.e., CX = 0
- **LOOPE/LOOPZ –** Used to loop a group of instructions till it satisfies ZF = 1 & CX = 0
- **LOOPNE/LOOPNZ –** Used to loop a group of instructions till it satisfies ZF = 0 & CX = 0
- **JCXZ –** Used to jump to the provided address if CX = 0

Interrupt Instructions

These instructions are used to call the interrupt during program execution.

- **INT** – Used to interrupt the program during execution and calling service specified.
- **INTO** – Used to interrupt the program during execution if OF = 1
- **IRET** – Used to return from interrupt service to the main program

THIRTEEN

MICROPROCESSOR - 8086 INTERRUPTS

Interrupt is the method of creating a temporary halt during program execution and allows peripheral devices to access the microprocessor. The microprocessor responds to that interrupt with an ISR (Interrupt Service Routine), which is a short program to instruct the microprocessor on how to handle the interrupt.

The following image shows the types of interrupts we have in a 8086 microprocessor –

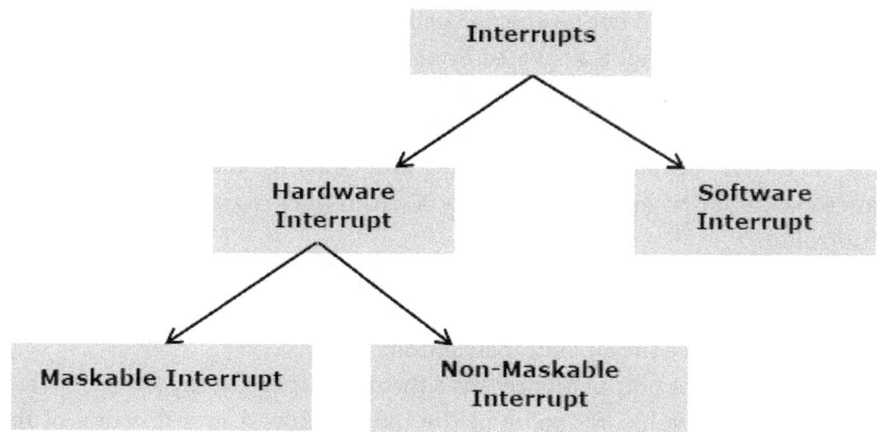

Hardware Interrupts

Hardware interrupt is caused by any peripheral device by sending a signal through a specified pin to the microprocessor.

The 8086 has two hardware interrupt pins, i.e. NMI and INTR. NMI is a non-maskable interrupt and INTR is a maskable interrupt having lower priority. One more interrupt pin associated is INTA called interrupt acknowledge.

NMI

It is a single non-maskable interrupt pin (NMI) having higher priority than the maskable interrupt request pin (INTR)and it is of type 2 interrupt.

When this interrupt is activated, these actions take place –

- Completes the current instruction that is in progress.
- Pushes the Flag register values on to the stack.
- Pushes the CS (code segment) value and IP (instruction pointer) value of the return address on to the stack.
- IP is loaded from the contents of the word location 00008H.
- CS is loaded from the contents of the next word location 0000AH.
- Interrupt flag and trap flag are reset to 0.

INTR

The INTR is a maskable interrupt because the microprocessor will be interrupted only if interrupts are enabled using set interrupt flag instruction. It should not be enabled using clear interrupt Flag instruction.

The INTR interrupt is activated by an I/O port. If the interrupt is enabled and NMI is disabled, then the microprocessor first completes the current execution and sends '0' on INTA pin twice. The first '0' means INTA informs the external device to get ready and during the second '0' the microprocessor receives the 8 bit, say X, from the programmable interrupt controller.

These actions are taken by the microprocessor –

- First completes the current instruction.
- Activates INTA output and receives the interrupt type, say X.
- Flag register value, CS value of the return address and IP value of the return address are pushed on to the stack.
- IP value is loaded from the contents of word location X × 4
- CS is loaded from the contents of the next word location.
- Interrupt flag and trap flag is reset to 0

Software Interrupts

Some instructions are inserted at the desired position into the program to create interrupts. These interrupt instructions can be used to test the working of various interrupt handlers. It includes –

INT- Interrupt instruction with type number

It is 2-byte instruction. First byte provides the op-code and the second byte provides the interrupt type number. There are 256 interrupt types under this group.

Its execution includes the following steps –

- Flag register value is pushed on to the stack.
- CS value of the return address and IP value of the return address are pushed on to the stack.
- IP is loaded from the contents of the word location 'type number' × 4
- CS is loaded from the contents of the next word location.
- Interrupt Flag and Trap Flag are reset to 0

The starting address for type0 interrupt is 000000H, for type1 interrupt is 00004H similarly for type2 is 00008H and ......so on. The first five pointers are dedicated interrupt pointers. i.e. –

- TYPE 0 interrupt represents division by zero situation.
- TYPE 1 interrupt represents single-step execution during the debugging of a program.
- TYPE 2 interrupt represents non-maskable NMI interrupt.
- TYPE 3 interrupt represents break-point interrupt.
- TYPE 4 interrupt represents overflow interrupt.

The interrupts from Type 5 to Type 31 are reserved for other advanced microprocessors, and interrupts from 32 to Type 255 are available for hardware and software interrupts.

INT 3-Break Point Interrupt Instruction

It is a 1-byte instruction having op-code is CCH. These instructions are inserted into the program so that when the processor reaches there, then it stops the normal execution of program and follows the break-point procedure.

Its execution includes the following steps –

- Flag register value is pushed on to the stack.
- CS value of the return address and IP value of the return address are pushed on to the stack.
- IP is loaded from the contents of the word location 3×4 = 0000CH
- CS is loaded from the contents of the next word location.
- Interrupt Flag and Trap Flag are reset to 0

INTO - Interrupt on overflow instruction

It is a 1-byte instruction and their mnemonic INTO. The op-code for this instruction is CEH. As the name suggests it is a conditional interrupt instruction, i.e. it is active only when the overflow flag is set to 1 and branches to the interrupt handler whose interrupt type number is 4. If the overflow flag is reset then, the execution continues to the next instruction.

Its execution includes the following steps –

- Flag register values are pushed on to the stack.
- CS value of the return address and IP value of the return address are pushed on to the stack.
- IP is loaded from the contents of word location 4×4 = 00010H
- CS is loaded from the contents of the next word location.
- Interrupt flag and Trap flag are reset to 0

FOURTEEN

MICROPROCESSOR - 8086 ADDRESSING MODES

The different ways in which a source operand is denoted in an instruction is known as addressing modes. There are 8 different addressing modes in 8086 programming –

Immediate addressing mode

The addressing mode in which the data operand is a part of the instruction itself is known as immediate addressing mode.

Example

MOV CX, 4929 H, ADD AX, 2387 H, MOV AL, FFH

Register addressing mode

It means that the register is the source of an operand for an instruction.

Example

MOV CX, AX ; copies the contents of the 16-bit AX register into ; the 16-bit CX register), ADD BX, AX

Direct addressing mode

The addressing mode in which the effective address of the memory location is written directly in the instruction.

Example

MOV AX, [1592H], MOV AL, [0300H]

Register indirect addressing mode

This addressing mode allows data to be addressed at any memory location through an offset address held in any of the following registers: BP,

BX, DI & SI.

Example

MOV AX, [BX] ; Suppose the register BX contains 4895H, then the contents ; 4895H are moved to AX ADD CX, {BX}

Based addressing mode

In this addressing mode, the offset address of the operand is given by the sum of contents of the BX/BP registers and 8-bit/16-bit displacement.

Example

MOV DX, [BX+04], ADD CL, [BX+08]

Indexed addressing mode

In this addressing mode, the operands offset address is found by adding the contents of SI or DI register and 8-bit/16-bit displacements.

Example

MOV BX, [SI+16], ADD AL, [DI+16]

Based-index addressing mode

In this addressing mode, the offset address of the operand is computed by summing the base register to the contents of an Index register.

Example

ADD CX, [AX+SI], MOV AX, [AX+DI]

Based indexed with displacement mode

In this addressing mode, the operands offset is computed by adding the base register contents. An Index registers contents and 8 or 16-bit displacement.

Example

MOV AX, [BX+DI+08], ADD CX, [BX+SI+16]

FIFTEEN

MULTIPROCESSOR CONFIGURATION OVERVIEW

Multiprocessor means a multiple set of processors that executes instructions simultaneously. There are three basic multiprocessor configurations.

- Coprocessor configuration
- Closely coupled configuration
- Loosely coupled configuration

Coprocessor Configuration

A Coprocessor is a specially designed circuit on microprocessor chip which can perform the same task very quickly, which the microprocessor performs. It reduces the work load of the main processor. The coprocessor shares the same memory, IO system, bus, control logic and clock generator. The coprocessor handles specialized tasks like mathematical calculations, graphical display on screen, etc.

The 8086 and 8088 can perform most of the operations but their instruction set is not able to perform complex mathematical operations, so in these cases the microprocessor requires the math coprocessor like Intel 8087 math coprocessor, which can easily perform these operations very quickly.

Block Diagram of Coprocessor Configuration:

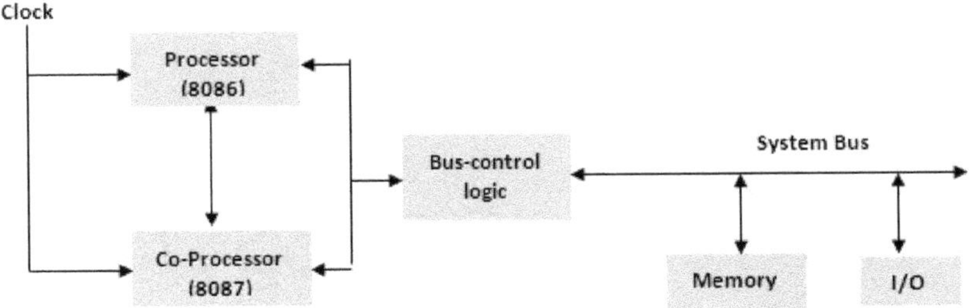

How is the coprocessor and the processor connected?

- The coprocessor and the processor is connected via TEST, RQ-/GT- and QS0 & QS1 signals.
- The TEST signal is connected to BUSY pin of coprocessor and the remaining 3 pins are connected to the coprocessor's 3 pins of the same name.
- TEST signal takes care of the coprocessor's activity, i.e. the coprocessor is busy or idle.
- The RT-/GT-is used for bus arbitration.
- The coprocessor uses QS0 & QS1 to track the status of the queue of the host processor.

Closely Coupled Configuration

Closely coupled configuration is similar to the coprocessor configuration, i.e. both share the same memory, I/O system bus, control logic, and control generator with the host processor. However, the coprocessor and the host processor fetches and executes their own instructions. The system bus is controlled by the coprocessor and the host processor independently.

Block Diagram of Closely Coupled Configuration:

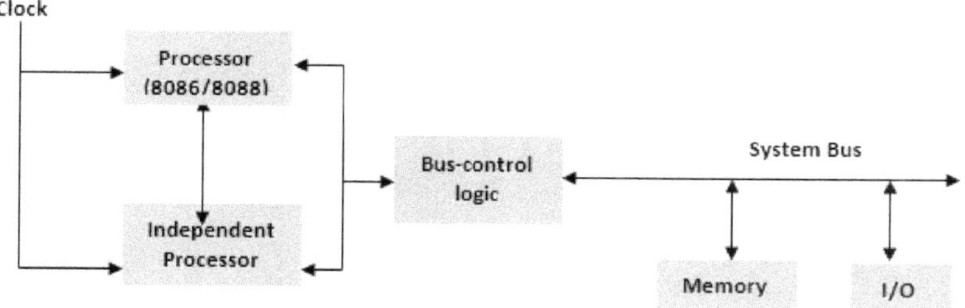

How is the processor and the independent processor connected?

- Communication between the host and the independent processor is done through memory space.
- None of the instructions are used for communication, like WAIT, ESC, etc.
- The host processor manages the memory and wakes up the independent processor by sending commands to one of its ports.
- Then the independent processor accesses the memory to execute the task.
- After completion of the task, it sends an acknowledgement to the host processor by using the status signal or an interrupt request.

Loosely Coupled Configuration

Loosely coupled configuration consists of the number of modules of the microprocessor based systems, which are connected through a common system bus. Each module consists of their own clock generator, memory, I/O devices and are connected through a local bus.

Block Diagram of Loosely Coupled Configuration:

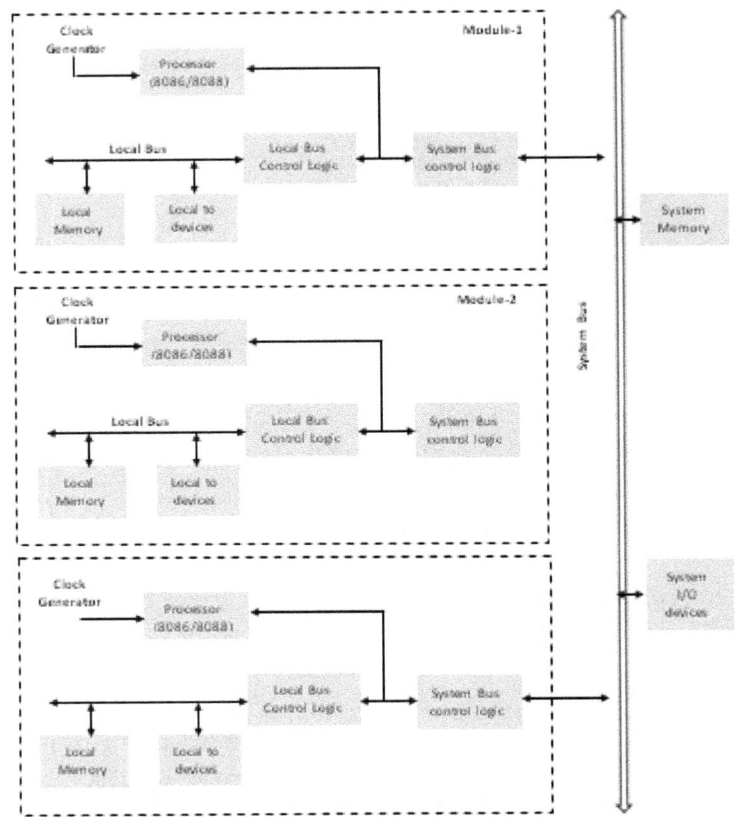

Advantages

- Having more than one processor results in increased efficiency.
- Each of the processors have their own local bus to access the local memory/I/O devices. This makes it easy to achieve parallel processing.
- The system structure is flexible, i.e. the failure of one module doesn't affect the whole system failure; faulty module can be replaced later.

SIXTEEN

8087 Numeric Data Processor

8087 numeric data processor is also known as Math co-processor, Numeric processor extension and Floating point unit. It was the first math coprocessor designed by Intel to pair with 8086/8088 resulting in easier and faster calculation.

Once the instructions are identified by the 8086/8088 processor, then it is allotted to the 8087 co-processor for further execution.

The data types supported by 8087 are –

- Binary Integers
- Packed decimal numbers
- Real numbers
- Temporary real format

The most prominent features of 8087 numeric data processor are as follows –

- It supports data of type integer, float, and real types ranging from 2-10 bytes.
- The processing speed is so high that it can calculate multiplication of two 64-bits real numbers in ~27 µs and can also calculate square-root in ~35 µs.
- It follows IEEE floating point standards.

8087 Architecture

8087 Architecture is divided into two groups, i.e., Control Unit (CU) and Numeric Extension Unit (NEU).

- The control unit handles all the communication between the processor and the memory such as it receives and decodes instructions, reads and writes memory operands, maintains parallel queue, etc. All the coprocessor instructions are ESC instructions, i.e., they start with 'F', the coprocessor only executes the ESC instructions while other instructions are executed by the microprocessor.
- The numeric extension unit handles all the numeric processor instructions like arithmetic, logical, transcendental, and data transfer instructions. It has 8 register stack, which holds the operands for instructions and their results.

The architecture of 8087 coprocessor is as follows –

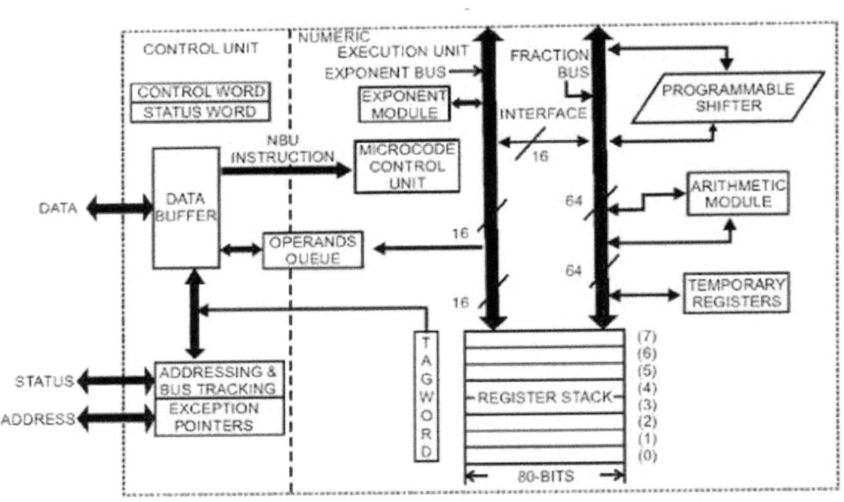

8087 Pin Description

Let us first take a look at the pin diagram of 8087 –

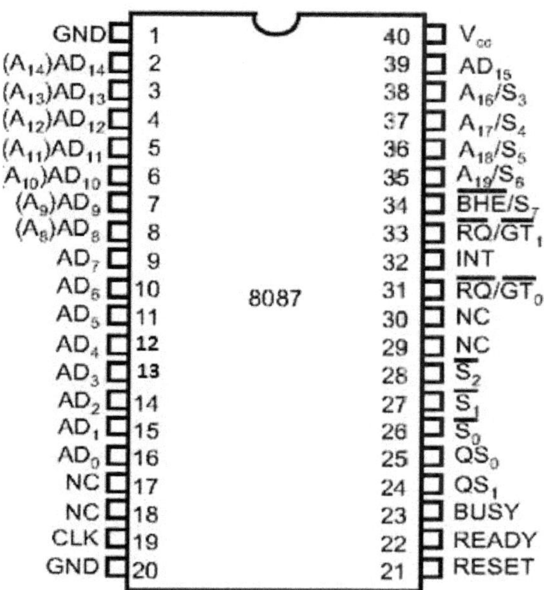

The following list provides the Pin Description of 8087 –

- AD0 – AD15 – These are the time multiplexed address/data lines, which carry addresses during the first clock cycle and data from the second clock cycle onwards.
- A19 / S6 – A16/S – These lines are the time multiplexed address/status lines. It functions in a similar way to the corresponding pins of 8086. The S6, S4 and S3 are permanently high, while the S5 is permanently low.
- BHE/S7 – During the first clock cycle, the BHE/S7 is used to enable data on to the higher byte of the 8086 data bus and after that works as status line S7.
- QS1, QS0 – These are queue status input signals which provides the status of instruction queue, their conditions as shown in the following table –

QS_0	QS_1	Status
0	0	No operation
0	1	First byte of opcode from the queue
1	0	Empty the queue
1	1	Subsequent byte from the queue

- INT – It is an interrupt signal, which changes to high when an unmasked exception has been received during the execution.
- BUSY – It is an output signal, when it is high it indicates a busy state to the CPU.
- READY – It is an input signal used to inform the coprocessor whether the bus is ready to receive data or not.
- RESET – It is an input signal used to reject the internal activities of the coprocessor and prepare it for further execution whenever required by the CPU.
- CLK – The CLK input provides the basic timings for the processor operation.
- VCC – It is a power supply signal, which requires +5V supply for the operation of the circuit.
- S0, S1, S2 – These are the status signals that provide the status of the operation which is used by the Bus Controller 8087 to generate memory and I/O control signals. These signals are active during the fourth clock cycle.

S_2	S_1	S_0	**Queue Status**
0	X	X	Unused
1	0	0	Unused
1	0	1	Memory read
1	1	0	Memory write
1	1	1	Passive

- RQ/GT1 & RQ/GT0 – These are the Request/Grant signals used by the 8087 processors to gain control of the bus from the host processor 8086/8088 for operand transfers.

SEVENTEEN

MICROCONTROLLERS - 8051

A microcontroller is a small and low-cost microcomputer, which is designed to perform the specific tasks of embedded systems like displaying microwave's information, receiving remote signals, etc.

The general microcontroller consists of the processor, the memory (RAM, ROM, EPROM), Serial ports, peripherals (timers, counters), etc.

Difference between Microprocessor and Microcontroller

The following table highlights the differences between a microprocessor and a microcontroller –

Microcontroller	Microprocessor
Microcontrollers are used to execute a single task within an application.	Microprocessors are used for big applications.
Its designing and hardware cost is low.	Its designing and hardware cost is high.
Easy to replace.	Not so easy to replace.
It is built with CMOS technology, which requires less power to operate.	Its power consumption is high because it has to control the entire system.
It consists of CPU, RAM, ROM, I/O ports.	It doesn't consist of RAM, ROM, I/O ports. It uses its pins to interface to peripheral devices.

Types of Microcontrollers

Microcontrollers are divided into various categories based on memory, architecture, bits and instruction sets. Following is the list of their types –

Bit

Based on bit configuration, the microcontroller is further divided into three categories.

- **8-bit microcontroller** – This type of microcontroller is used to execute arithmetic and logical operations like addition, subtraction, multiplication division, etc. For example, Intel 8031 and 8051 are 8 bits microcontroller.
- **16-bit microcontroller** – This type of microcontroller is used to perform arithmetic and logical operations where higher accuracy and performance is required. For example, Intel 8096 is a 16-bit microcontroller.
- **32-bit microcontroller** – This type of microcontroller is generally used in automatically controlled appliances like automatic operational machines, medical appliances, etc.

Memory

Based on the memory configuration, the microcontroller is further divided into two categories.

- **External memory microcontroller** – This type of microcontroller is designed in such a way that they do not have a program memory on the chip. Hence, it is named as external memory microcontroller. For example: Intel 8031 microcontroller.
- **Embedded memory microcontroller** – This type of microcontroller is designed in such a way that the microcontroller has all programs and data memory, counters and timers, interrupts, I/O ports are embedded on the chip. For example: Intel 8051 microcontroller.

Instruction Set

Based on the instruction set configuration, the microcontroller is further divided into two categories.

- **CISC** – CISC stands for complex instruction set computer. It allows the user to insert a single instruction as an alternative to many simple instructions.
- **RISC** – RISC stands for Reduced Instruction Set Computers. It reduces the operational time by shortening the clock cycle per instruction.

Applications of Microcontrollers

- Microcontrollers are widely used in various different devices such as –
- Light sensing and controlling devices like LED.
- Temperature sensing and controlling devices like microwave oven, chimneys.
- Fire detection and safety devices like Fire alarm.
- Measuring devices like Volt Meter.

Microcontrollers - 8051 Architecture

8051 microcontroller is designed by Intel in 1981. It is an 8-bit microcontroller. It is built with 40 pins DIP (dual inline package), 4kb of ROM storage and 128 bytes of RAM storage, 2 16-bit timers. It consists of are four parallel 8-bit ports, which are programmable as well as addressable as per the requirement. An on-chip crystal oscillator is integrated in the microcontroller having crystal frequency of 12 MHz.

Let us now discuss the architecture of 8051 Microcontroller.

In the architecture diagram, the system bus connects all the support devices to the CPU. The system bus consists of an 8-bit data bus, a 16-bit address bus and bus control signals. All other devices like program memory, ports, data memory, serial interface, interrupt control, timers, and the CPU are all interfaced together through the system bus.

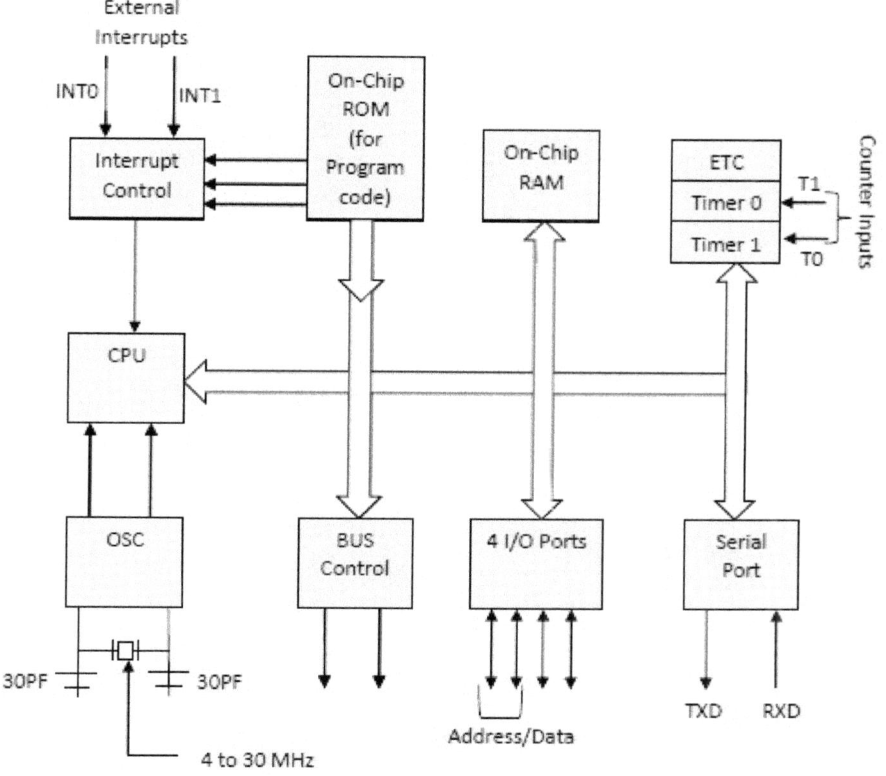

Microcontrollers - 8051 Pin Description

The pin diagram of 8051 microcontroller looks as follows –

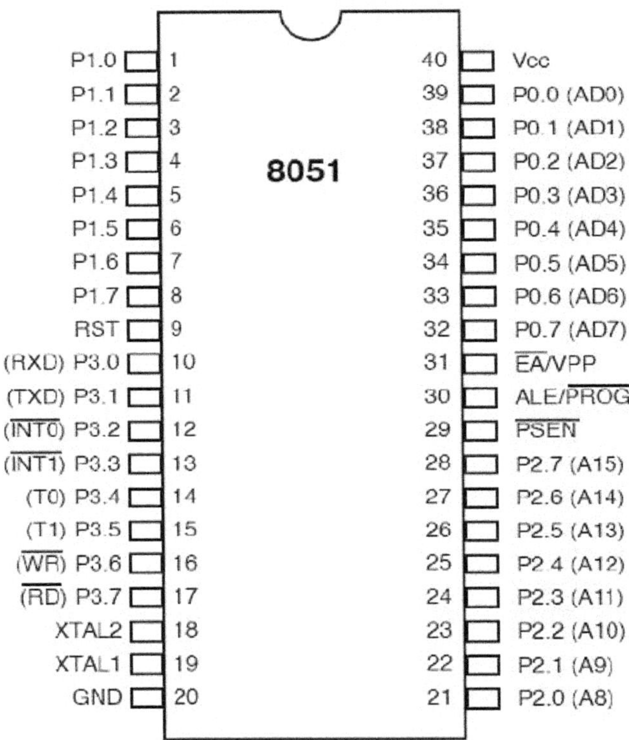

- **Pins 1 to 8 –** These pins are known as Port 1. This port doesn't serve any other functions. It is internally pulled up, bi-directional I/O port.
- **Pin 9 –** It is a RESET pin, which is used to reset the microcontroller to its initial values.
- **Pins 10 to 17 –** These pins are known as Port 3. This port serves some functions like interrupts, timer input, control signals, serial communication signals RxD and TxD, etc.
- **Pins 18 & 19 –** These pins are used for interfacing an external crystal to get the system clock.
- **Pin 20 –** This pin provides the power supply to the circuit.
- **Pins 21 to 28 –** These pins are known as Port 2. It serves as I/O port. Higher order address bus signals are also multiplexed using this port.

- **Pin 29 –** This is PSEN pin which stands for Program Store Enable. It is used to read a signal from the external program memory.
- **Pin 30 –** This is EA pin which stands for External Access input. It is used to enable/disable the external memory interfacing.
- **Pin 31 –** This is ALE pin which stands for Address Latch Enable. It is used to demultiplex the address-data signal of port.
- **Pins 32 to 39 –** These pins are known as Port 0. It serves as I/O port. Lower order address and data bus signals are multiplexed using this port.
- **Pin 40 –** This pin is used to provide power supply to the circuit.

Microcontrollers 8051 Input Output Ports

8051 microcontrollers have 4 I/O ports each of 8-bit, which can be configured as input or output. Hence, total 32 input/output pins allow the microcontroller to be connected with the peripheral devices.

Pin configuration, i.e. the pin can be configured as 1 for input and 0 for output as per the logic state.

- **Input/Output (I/O) pin –** All the circuits within the microcontroller must be connected to one of its pins except P0 port because it does not have pull-up resistors built-in.
- **Input pin –** Logic 1 is applied to a bit of the P register. The output FE transistor is turned off and the other pin remains connected to the power supply voltage over a pull-up resistor of high resistance.

Port 0 – The P0 (zero) port is characterized by two functions –

- When the external memory is used then the lower address byte (addresses A0A7) is applied on it, else all bits of this port are configured as input/output.
- When P0 port is configured as an output then other ports consisting of pins with built-in pull-up resistor connected by its end to 5V power supply, the pins of this port have this resistor left out.

Input Configuration

If any pin of this port is configured as an input, then it acts as if it "floats", i.e. the input has unlimited input resistance and in-determined potential.

Output Configuration

When the pin is configured as an output, then it acts as an "open drain". By applying logic 0 to a port bit, the appropriate pin will be connected to ground (0V), and applying logic 1, the external output will keep on "floating".

In order to apply logic 1 (5V) on this output pin, it is necessary to build an external pullup resistor.

Port 1

P1 is a true I/O port as it doesn't have any alternative functions as in P0, but this port can be configured as general I/O only. It has a built-in pull-up resistor and is completely compatible with TTL circuits.

Port 2

P2 is similar to P0 when the external memory is used. Pins of this port occupy addresses intended for the external memory chip. This port can be used for higher address byte with addresses A8-A15. When no memory is added then this port can be used as a general input/output port similar to Port 1.

Port 3

In this port, functions are similar to other ports except that the logic 1 must be applied to appropriate bit of the P3 register.

Pins Current Limitations

- When pins are configured as an output (i.e. logic 0), then the single port pins can receive a current of 10mA.
- When these pins are configured as inputs (i.e. logic 1), then built-in pull-up resistors provide very weak current, but can activate up to 4 TTL inputs of LS series.
- If all 8 bits of a port are active, then the total current must be limited to 15mA (port P0: 26mA).
- If all ports (32 bits) are active, then the total maximum current must be limited to 71mA.

EIGHTEEN

MICROCONTROLLERS - 8051 INTERRUPTS

Interrupts are the events that temporarily suspend the main program, pass the control to the external sources and execute their task. It then passes the control to the main program where it had left off.

8051 has 5 interrupt signals, i.e. INT0, TFO, INT1, TF1, RI/TI. Each interrupt can be enabled or disabled by setting bits of the IE register and the whole interrupt system can be disabled by clearing the EA bit of the same register.

IE (Interrupt Enable) Register

This register is responsible for enabling and disabling the interrupt. EA register is set to one for enabling interrupts and set to 0 for disabling the interrupts. Its bit sequence and their meanings are shown in the following figure.

EA	-	-	ES	ET1	EX1	ET0	EX0

EA	IE.7	It disables all interrupts. When EA = 0 no interrupt will be acknowledged and EA = 1 enables the interrupt individually.
-	IE.6	Reserved for future use.
-	IE.5	Reserved for future use.
ES	IE.4	Enables/disables serial port interrupt.
ET1	IE.3	Enables/disables timer1 overflow interrupt.
EX1	IE.2	Enables/disables external interrupt1.
ET0	IE.1	Enables/disables timer0 overflow interrupt.
EX0	IE.0	Enables/disables external interrupt0.

IP (Interrupt Priority) Register

We can change the priority levels of the interrupts by changing the corresponding bit in the Interrupt Priority (IP) register as shown in the following figure.

- A low priority interrupt can only be interrupted by the high priority interrupt, but not interrupted by another low priority interrupt.
- If two interrupts of different priority levels are received simultaneously, the request of higher priority level is served.
- If the requests of the same priority levels are received simultaneously, then the internal polling sequence determines which request is to be serviced.

-	-	PT2	PS	PT1	PX1	PT0	PX0
bit7	bit6	bit5	bit4	bit3	bit2	bit1	

-	IP.6	Reserved for future use.
-	IP.5	Reserved for future use.
PS	IP.4	It defines the serial port interrupt priority level.
PT1	IP.3	It defines the timer interrupt of 1 priority.
PX1	IP.2	It defines the external interrupt priority level.
PT0	IP.1	It defines the timer0 interrupt priority level.
PX0	IP.0	It defines the external interrupt of 0 priority level.

TCON Register

TCON register specifies the type of external interrupt to the microcontroller.

At A Glance

In this book we discussed about microprocessor 8085 and 8086. Their architectural description alongwith infacing devices. Apart from microprocessor we have studied about microcontroller 8051 as well.

This book is designed for all those students pursing their Bachelor's degree in Electronics & Communication Engineering and Electrical Engineering. It will help them understand the basic concepts related to Microprocessors and microcontroller.

In this book, all the topics have been explained from elementary level. Therefore, a beginner can understand the topics very easily.

About The Author

Kh. Kamal Ahmed

Currently posted in Dumka Engineering College, Jharkhand, as an Assistant Professor in the department of Electronics & Communication Engineering since 2015. Previously posted in Techno Global Balurghat as an Assistant Professor in Electronics & Communication Engineering Department from 2014-2015.

Completed M.Tech in Communication Engineering from Netaji Subhash Engineering College in 2013 under WBUT(Presently known as MAKAUT) and B.Tech in Electronics & Tele-Communication Engineering from Balasore College of Engineering & Technology in 2011 under BPUT.

Other Book(s):

INTERNET OF THINGS

www.ingramcontent.com/pod-product-compliance
Ingram Content Group UK Ltd.
Pitfield, Milton Keynes, MK11 3LW, UK
UKHW021912190726
13853UKWH00002B/631